Apostles of the Culture of Life

APOSTLES
OF THE
CULTURE OF LIFE

Dr. Donald T. DeMarco

TAN Books
Charlotte, North Carolina

Cover design by Caroline K. Green

Library of Congress Control Number: 2018954433

ISBN: 978-1-5051-1325-9

Published in the United States by
TAN Books
PO Box 410487
Charlotte, NC 28241
www.TANBooks.com

Printed and bound in the United States of America

More Praise for *Apostles of the Culture of Life* . . .

"DeMarco here provides 56 vignettes of those heroes from different walks of life who stood up and said "no" to abortion-on-demand and euthanasia as a supposed merciful act. His broad interests and deep understanding will uplift readers with inspiring and inspired examples of those who saw the evil of deliberate medicalized killing and responded with reason, courage, and love."

—Paul Tuns, author and editor of *Interim*

"Dr. DeMarco shows that the struggle to support life in the face of numerous attacks is heroically evident among people from many disciplines and religions. This superb book is a valuable addition to the library of anyone who preaches, teaches, or speaks on issues related to the defense of life."

—Dr. Cynthia Toolin-Wilson, Academic Dean of Online Learning, Holy Apostles College and Seminary

"In this new work, Don DeMarco manages to acquaint us with each 'apostle of life' as if for the first time, while, at the same time inspiring us to emulate them. A most uplifting and encouraging work!"

—Christine Valentine-Owsik, Editor of *Legatus Magazine*

"Donald DeMarco has written an amazingly detailed account of the many prominent people who have borne the brunt of the pro-life movement over the years. I had never before realized the far-ranging variety of the movement and all the heroic people who have sustained it."

—James Hitchcock, Professor Emeritus, St. Louis University

"Here is a unique and valuable work that celebrates and brings to life the achievements of the many heroes who are truly *Apostles of the Culture of Life*."

—Stephen D. Schwarz, godson of Dietrich von Hildebrand and author of *Understanding Abortion: From Mixed Feelings to Rational Thought*

"I have always said that it would have been a cheerful experience for me as a university student to have been in one of Professor DeMarco's classes, soaking in his wisdom. It is an honor for me to be listed in the burgeoning group of lovers of life and light Professor DeMarco defines as *Apostles for the Culture of Life*."

—Judie Brown, President of American Life League

This book is respectfully dedicated to the memory of Jim McFadden:
Apostle of Life, Beacon of Light

Contents

Acknowledgments

I want to thank Peggy Moen of *The Wanderer*, Tom Wehner of the *National Catholic Register*, Judie Brown of *Celebrate Life*, Christine Owsik of *Legatus*, Maria Maffucci and Anne Conlon of the *Human Life Review*, and the editors of *Human Life International* for granting permission to publish many (but not all) of the articles originally published, though under different titles, of significantly different lengths, in pre-revised forms, and sometimes with a different focus. In addition, some of these articles were further revised after consulting with featured individuals. These editors contributed greatly in planting and cultivating the seed which ultimately grew and became adapted to *Apostles of the Culture of Life*.

Foreword

At the *Human Life Review*, we look forward to submissions from the prolific Professor Donald DeMarco. We know his prose will be philosophically rich and morally astute, and it won't be *just* these great and good things: there will also likely be some delightful surprises. It might be a new way of understanding a concept, a humorous anecdote or bit of whimsy, or a fascinating cultural reference—to baseball, music, science, or historical curiosities. And encompassing it all, a compassionate understanding of human nature and unwavering support for the sanctity of life.

This is an apt description of the book you are holding: *Apostles of the Culture of Life*. It's a collection of brief biographies of an eclectic group of human beings, some living, some recently deceased, and some who lived centuries ago. What binds them all together is that they are "heroes" in the "pervasive conflict between the Culture of Life and the Culture of Death." Included here are philosophers, doctors, athletes, performers, composers, writers, comedians, theologians, great Catholic saints and even the Holy Family. Each portrait is enriched by colorful details. For example, in "A

Doctor of Love," we learn about the Australian Dr. John Billings, a pioneer in discovering methods of natural family planning, and we also learn something poignant about mother kangaroos and the "instinctive wisdom" found in nature.

DeMarco kindly dedicated this book to my late father, J. P. McFadden—profiled in "Piety and Laughter"—one of the individuals lesser-known to the world, but well-known to fellow soldiers in the early days of the pro-life movement. When J. P. died in October of 1998, *New York Post* columnist Ray Kerrison wrote (in "Death Takes a Stubborn Defender of Life") that J. P. "did not build skyscrapers or write his name in Broadway neon. He didn't run City Hall or preside over a corporate empire." He "was a rock of a man who served God, family and country" and devoted most of his working life to protecting human life. While some of the apostles here might have had their names in neon—Clare Boothe Luce comes to mind—and some were famous, that is not what matters here. What connects them all is their heroic witness to the truth of human dignity and purpose.

Today, praise God, there is tremendous youthful energy in the pro-life movement. These new soldiers need to get this book and learn the stories of those who forged the noble path they now follow. To life!

Maria McFadden Maffucci

Preface

It is an unchallengeable axiom that a war cannot be won without heroes. The war of which I am speaking, one that is raging presently, is not military, but cultural. And although it is essentially cultural, rivers of blood, nonetheless, continue to flow. It is the pervasive conflict between the Culture of Life and the Culture of Death. And it is a most unfortunate aspect of this war that the Mass Media, which shapes the popular mind to such a large degree, neither honors nor admires the heroes who are working for the Culture of Life.

Roger Rosenblatt, a veteran journalist of the *Washington Post, Life, Time,* and the *New York Times,* has stated, in a moment of candor, "My trade in journalism is sodden these days with practitioners who seem incapable of admiring others or anything." Celebrity replaces character; success outshines sanctity; virtuosity eclipses virtue. Tabloids feast on gossip. Scandals are more newsworthy than acts of philanthropy.

The "Hall of Fame for Great Americans," the first of its kind, located in New York City and founded in 1990, is largely forgotten. It took nineteen years to raise the $25,000 to commission the bust of Franklin Delano Roosevelt. By contrast, the Rock and Roll Hall of Fame in Cleveland, Ohio, founded in 1995, has hosted more than ten million visitors and has had a cumulative economic impact estimated at more than $1.8 billion. The best-selling postage stamps feature Elvis Presley and Marilyn Monroe. Lady Gaga and Madonna are household names. WrestleMania III drew a world indoor attendance record of 93,173 fans.

Peter H. Gibbon, Senior Research Fellow at Boston University's School of Education is the author of *A Call to Heroism – Renewing America's Vision of Greatness*. He claims that "in an age of instant communication, in which there is little time for reflection, accuracy, balance or integrity—the media creates the impression that sleaze is everywhere, that nothing is sacred, that no one is noble, and that there are no heroes." But there are heroes. It is just that they are either suppressed or forgotten.

I refer to pro-life heroes in this gallery of heroes as "apostles" because their acts of heroism include delivering a message to society that is as vitally important as it is politically incorrect. We need to know who these great "Apostles of Life" are, what they have done, and the meaning of their message. We need to bring them out from cultural concealment and into the public light.

They come from many walks of life: medicine, philosophy, theology, the arts, sports, politics, and from the world at large. Their lives and contributions should be inspirations for every person of good will. Though highly diverse in their backgrounds and specific talents, they all agree on the inherent goodness of life and the need to express that conviction on a personal and social level no matter what obstacles lie in their path.

Writing about these "Apostles of Life" is a most humbling experience. My modest role as a writer does not require heroism. It is, by comparison with true heroes, a relatively undemanding task. At the same time, it does require an appreciation for the role of the apostle; that is, the one who brings the message to the world that life is a great gift and that respect for life is a joyful obligation. The forty-two extraordinary individuals whose profiles appear on the following pages are not only "Apostles of Life" but also "Beacons of Light." This book, then, is about the radical importance of both "life" and "light," and the message its apostles bring to a Culture of Death that routinely devalues life and commonly denies light.

June 13, 2017

Kitchener, Ontario

Part I

Apostles From the World of Medicine

Jérôme Lejeune

I first met Dr. Jérôme Lejeune at a pro-life conference in Montreal. Just minutes before his scheduled presentation to a large and expectant audience, we, along with several other participants, were tending to our ablutions in the men's lavatory. Since it is not practical to wash one's hands while holding a portfolio of notes, we naturally set them aside until our momentary task was completed. When we were ready to leave, however, we inadvertently picked up the wrong ones. Dr. Lejeune was the first to realize the mishap and, observing a man leaving the washroom with a folder that looked suspiciously like his own, said, without the lightest trace of anxiety in his voice, "That gentleman is leaving with my notes." I quickly made the embarrassing discovery that it was I who had Lejeune's notes (and he, mine). While exchanging folders I complimented him on how, even in the face of a potentially embarrassing moment, he remained the picture of calmness and the essence of a gentleman.

If the expression "a gentleman and a scholar" ever had a

perfect witness, it was Jérôme Lejeune. He was a world-renowned geneticist who discovered the genetic origin of Down syndrome (trisomy 21). This discovery was the first time that a defect in intellectual development was shown to be traced to a chromosomal abnormality. It was a major breakthrough and opened the door to the discoveries of monosomy 9, trisomy 13, and other links between a genetic disorder and a physiological aberration. Perhaps cures could be on the horizon. Lejeune made the comment in the medical journal *Lancet* that curing children of Down syndrome may not be far away "if only the disease is attacked, not the babies."

But he was far more than a brilliant researcher. "Our intelligence," he once stated, "is not an abstract machine; it is also incarnate, and the heart is as important as the faculty of reason, or more precisely, reason is nothing without the heart." His gentlemanly affection extended to all human beings, including the Down dyndrome community and frozen embryos. He was pro-life, thoroughly, totally, and consistently.

He was invited to be an expert witness in a court case involving the disposition of seven frozen embryos. A dispute arose in a divorce court in which the wife wanted her tiny offspring to live while the husband wanted them to be destroyed. Lejeune, at his own expense, flew to the small town in Tennessee to provide scientific testimony in behalf of the humanity of the frozen embryos. The town was Maryville, the mother's name was Mary, and her lawyer's name was Christenberry, a striking coincidence that was not lost on Dr. Lejeune. He hastened to assist what he referred to as the "Seven Hopes of Mary." "If the judgment of Solomon which is pronounced only twice every three thousand

years, occurs during your lifetime," he remarked, "it's worth
a detour." A full account of the Maryville trial is contained
in Lejeune's book *The Concentration Can*.[1]

Lejeune's scientific testimony proved successful. Judge
Dale Young rendered his decision which recognized that
the embryos were not the property of anyone since they are
members of the human family. He concluded, "The person
who should have custody of the children is the person who
intends to preserve the life of the children." His decision
was, indeed, Solomonic.

The good doctor's affirmation of the right to live, while
honored by many, was strongly denounced by others. At the
United Nations, a debate took place in which most of those
present approved abortion. The usual rationalizations were
offered: the prevention of deformed infants, the mortality
rate from clandestine abortions, sparing women from psychological suffering, and so on. Lejeune, alone in his camp,
raised a politically incorrect protest, "Here we have an institute of health that is turning into an institute of death."
That evening he wrote to his wife, confiding in her that "this
afternoon I lost my Nobel Prize."

The calumny that was visited upon Lejeune extended to
his five children. Clara Lejeune, Jérôme's daughter, testifies
to this in her biography of her father, *Life is a Blessing*. She
recalls the frightful graffiti on the outside walls of the medical school: "Tremble, Lejeune! The MLAC [a revolution-
ary student movement] is watching. Lejeune is an assassin.

---

[1]   Jérôme Lejeune, *The Concentration Can: When Does Human Life
       Begin?: An Eminent Geneticist Testifies* (San Francisco: Ignatius
       Press, 1992).

Kill Lejeune! Or else: Lejeune and his little monsters must die." Such words, writes Clara, "brought our childhood very quickly to an end. These are things that cannot be forgotten even if, during adolescence, there is a sort of play-acting in these street wars, the seriousness of which is not realized."

Jérôme Lejeune passed away on Easter Sunday, 1994, at the all-too-young age of sixty-seven, thirty-three days after he had been appointed president of the Pontifical Academy for Life. As his daughter recounts, he had been inspired by the final line of Brahms's *German Requiem*, "Blessed are those who die in the Lord, for their works follow them." His close friend, Pope John Paul II, upon hearing of "the death of our brother Jérôme," had these words to say: "May the truth about life be also a source of spiritual strength for the family of the deceased, for the Church in France, and for all of us, to whom Professor Lejeune has left the truly brilliant witness of his life as a man and as a Christian."

What did it matter that a journalist writing for the weekly newspaper *Charlie Hebdo* labelled Lejeune as "an enemy of the worst kind"? The truth and accomplishments of Lejeune will live on. Shortly after his passing, a petition appeared in *Le Monde* signed by three thousand physicians demanding recognition for the embryo as a member of the human species, and not to be exploited for manipulations of any kind.

During his visit to Paris for world Youth Day, John Paul II visited the grave of Jérôme Jean Louis Marie Lejeune. The Catholic Church has named Lejeune "Servant of God," and the Abbey of Saint Wandrille in France has inaugurated his cause for sainthood.

A Doctor of Love

John Billings

D r. Charles Norris, a retired obstetrician/gynecologist, has said of Dr. John Billings that "he will go down in the annals of medical research as one of the greatest medical researchers of our time for his pioneering work in modern methods of natural family planning." Georgetown University honored Dr. Billings with its President's Medal. In addition, he was elevated to the Fellowship of the Australian College of Physicians and, on the recommendation of Queen Elizabeth II, was appointed a member of the Order of Australia. He was made Knight Commander of St. Gregory by Pope Paul VI and similarly honored later by Pope John Paul II. Dr. Billings was the recipient of numerous honors and accolades from several universities. Pope Benedict described the Australian pioneer as a "noble soul."

Dr. Billings was certainly a man of science. More than that, however, he was a man of love. In an address he gave in April 2000, he reminisced about his wife and their marriage: "My mind goes back to that time, now sixty-two years ago, when I saw a beautiful young woman smiling at her friends in the dissecting room of the Anatomy School at the University of Melbourne and thought immediately, 'I would love to spend my life with that woman if she could come to love me.'" His marriage in 1943 to Evelyn Thomas, who reciprocated his love, lasted until his death in 2007. Their sixty-three-year romance bore nine children and prepared the way for thirty-seven grandchildren and twenty-seven great-grandchildren: a life legacy *par excellence*. "There is no reason at all to be afraid of babies," Dr. John was happy to announce.

Meeting the Billings was like being adopted into a loving family. Among their many acts of hospitality was taking me to the Healesville Sanctuary, just outside of Melbourne, where, for the first time in my life, I got to pet a kangaroo. Lyn explained to me that kangaroos are not particularly intelligent, though they do make good pets. Sometimes a very young kangaroo (a joey) is found in the woods, having been tossed out of its mother's pouch while she is fleeing from a dingo. As Lyn continued to explain, the mother knows that she cannot outrun her predator and so she does the only thing she can do to save the life of her offspring. Nature has an instinctive wisdom that is sometimes lost on human beings. Dr. John was fond of quoting a passage from St. Thomas Aquinas in which the Angelic Doctor stated that he had two and only two sources of knowledge that he could trust as representing the truth, those being Nature and Scripture. The two doctors went beyond graciousness when they reviewed a forthcoming book of mine, *New Perspectives in Contraception*, and penned a complimentary foreword.

John Billings had a special affection for poetry and introduced to me the Australian poet James McAuley, a communist who eventually became a Catholic. In one of his poems, McAuley expresses a sentiment that was particularly meaningful for Billings who tried as best he could to bring some measure of good into the world. It is a poem called "Retreat," about Divine Providence that offers hope for those who do not see the good fruits of their good efforts:

> Nor is failure our disgrace:
> By ways we cannot know
> He keeps the merit in his hand,
> And suddenly as no one planned,
> Behold the kingdom grow!

In an address Billings gave in Madras, India in 1997, he began by alluding to a fact of nature that is an ineradicable part of our being. "Deep in the heart of every human being is the desire to live in an environment of justice, peace, and love. It is therefore not difficult for us to perceive that we are living in a sick world." The world had become the doctor's patient and he was not afraid to diagnose its ills truthfully. "We need to change human hearts," he went on to say, "so that the rights of all individuals will be recognized, respected and defended. . . . All the rights of human persons depend primarily on the fundamental right to life, upon which all other rights can be defined."

Dr. Billings, as a good doctor, made few if any concessions to political correctness or false bromides. He strongly opposed the erroneous assumption that condoms provide an effective prevention against the transmission of the AIDS virus. He pointed out that although the use of the condom will lower the incidence of AIDS in a single case, repeated sexual activities with the condom, according to statistical evidence, will eventually reach the same transmission level as in instances where the condom is not used. People disregard the laws of nature at their peril.

In 1953, Dr. John began working on a method of natural family planning that involved observing specific indicators of fertility and infertility. He gradually focused on the changes to cervical mucus patterns of sensation that could be readily detected by a woman who wanted to achieve or avoid pregnancy. Although Dr. John Billings maintained his career as a consulting neurologist to St. Vincent's Hospital, he and his wife spent a large part of each year traveling to other countries, training teachers in the Billings Ovulation Method, lecturing to doctors and students, and establishing teaching centers. Their method was approved by the Catholic Church and was adopted by the World Health Organization. It was the only natural method of family planning accepted by the Chinese government.

The Billings were close friends with Mother Teresa and spent much time with her. When she passed away in 2007, John wrote a tribute to her, *In Memoriam—Mother Teresa of Calcutta*, in which he quoted another very good friend of the now sainted nun, Malcolm Muggeridge: "I can only say of her that in a dark time she is a burning shining light; in a cruel time, a living embodiment of Christ's gospel of love; in a godless time, the Word dwelling among us, full of grace and truth. For this, all who have the inestimable privilege of knowing her, or knowing of her, must be eternally grateful."

Dr. John Billings died at aged eighty-nine on April 1, 2007, at an aged care center after a long illness. His widow, Dr. Evelyn Billings, died on February 16, 2013 at the age of ninety-five, following a brief illness. *Sic transit gloria mundi.*

FATHER OF THE PRO-LIFE MOVEMENT

Jack Willke

O n Friday, February 20, 2015, at eighty-nine years of age, Dr. Jack Willke passed into a world where abortions do not take place. He and his wife, Barbara, are regarded as the parents of the pro-life movement. Their *Handbook on Abortion*[2] has sold an estimated 1.5 million copies. Coupled with their later work, *Abortion: Questions and Answers*,[3] the tandem has been translated into thirty-two languages. Altogether, the couple authored twelve books on human sexuality and abortion. They frequently appeared together on radio and TV shows and delivered their pro-life message personally in sixty-four different countries.

It has been said that when a person who has enjoyed a rich and generous life passes away, he should inspire expressions of gratitude rather than grief. Jack Willke lived a full life

---

[2] J. C. and Barbara Willke, *Handbook on Abortion* (Cincinnati: Hayes Publishing Co., 1976).

[3] John C. Willke, *Abortion Questions & Answers: Love Them Both* (Cincinnati, Ohio: Hayes Pub. Co., 2003).

and his work has benefitted millions. His death did, indeed, sadden me, but it also brought back some happy memories.

The year was 1972, and Dr. Jack Willke was coming to my home town of Kitchener, Ontario. I was chosen to interview him on our local television station. On the night prior to the telecast, a philosopher friend and I poured through pro-abortion literature in search of the dumbest reasons we could find that supported the pro-abortion cause. I wanted Dr. Willke to look good (and the other side to look bad). When he arrived at the studio, I was already seated on the set so that we did not have a chance to exchange pleasantries. A few pro-abortion advocates sat in the audience, eager to hear how the interview would go. I don't think I needed to go the extra mile to make my guest look good. He sparkled, with his kind demeanor and razor-sharp mind. What I did not expect, however, is that ombudsmen in the audience thought that *I* looked good. Consequently, they wanted to recruit me to appear in a program that promoted their view. This surprising invitation took me completely off stride. How could such bad arguments look so good from the other side?

Convinced that I was ignorant on the issue, the kindly doctor armed me with pictures of aborted fetuses and a great deal of pertinent literature. Still, at that point, I had not shown my hand. I welcomed his concern and generosity and I knew that I could keep the charade going as long as he saw me as convertible. A couple of years later, my first book came out: *Abortion in Perspective: The Rose Palace or the Fiery*

Furnace.[4] It included much of the valuable information the good doctor had prescribed for me.

After the show, I drove Dr. Willke and his wife to my house where my wife had prepared a lasagna lunch. *En route,* I said something which I like to think was clever but has forever slipped from my memory bank. Whatever I said worked and my distinguished guest expressed relief that he did not have to dine with people who were not on the side of life. He did not say the word *kooks,* but that is how I read his mind. Now he could look forward to digesting a meal comfortably without worrying about the peculiar moral views of his hosts.

My daughter, Jocelyn, was four years young at the time. Jack sat her on his knee, whereupon she sang, without the slightest sign of self-consciousness, the "Evening Prayer" from *Hansel and Gretel* ("When at night I go to bed/Fourteen Angels watch my head"). This is the most popular aria ever composed by the possessor of the most comical and cumbersome name in all operatic literature—Engelbert Humperdinck. Jack was more than charmed. Could he have imagined at that time that this beguiling songstress would be mother to four little songstresses of her own?

This moment of unexpected music is a cherished memory. Looking back, I viewed it as an interesting reversal of roles. Dr. Willke was used to lecturing to a large audience. This time, in my home, he was the sole member of an audience of one. He had doffed the teacher's hat and was happy

---

4   Donald DeMarco, *Abortion in Perspective: The Rose Palace or the Fiery Dragon?* (Cincinnati: Hiltz & Hayes, 1982).

to be serenaded by a four-year-old. He was father to six (and grandfather to twenty-two), and I viewed his performance as a step-father to one as something for which he was well prepared.

John Charles Willke was born in Maria Stein, Ohio on April 5, 1925. He was both the son and grandson of medical doctors. He earned his MD from the University of Cincinnati and was a practicing obstetrician in Cincinnati from 1950 until 1988 when he retired from his practice to engage in pro-life work fulltime. He was president of National Right to Life, America's oldest and largest pro-life organization, from 1984 through 1991. He founded the Life Issues Institute in 1991 and is credited with converting President George Bush from a pro-choice to a pro-life position on abortion.

Willke's philosophy was a model of simplicity. He firmly believed that science and common sense would be enough to change minds. He offered empirical and scientific evidence that the unborn child is a human being and that abortion is a form of killing. "This is a unique being, containing within itself a genetic package, completely programmed for and actively moving toward adult human existence," he would explain to his audience. "It has, by any standard, a life of its own and in no way is part of the mother or father."

Jack Willke was not without political affiliations. Mitt Romney's presidential campaign in 2008 endorsed Dr. Willke as "an important surrogate for Governor Romney's pro-life and pro-family agenda." Romney himself stated that he was pleased to "have the support of a man who has meant so much to the pro-life movement in our country."

The final project of Dr. Willke and his wife is an auto-biographical account of their pro-life work, *Abortion and the Pro-life Movement, An Inside View.*[5] Dr. Jack Willke will surely be missed, but his legacy has been firmly established. Personally, I like to think that as he entered the pearly gates he was serenaded by fourteen angels.

---

[5]   J. C. Willke, Barbara Willke, and Marie Willke Meyers, *Abortion and the Pro-Life Movement: An Inside View* (West Conshohocken, PA : Infinity Publishing, 2014).

Karl Stern

Some years ago, I had the privilege of meeting the distinguished Thomistic philosopher Josef Pieper. I knew of his relationship with Karl Stern. When I informed him of Stern's passing, he was saddened, but directly recalled how beautifully his dear friend played Schubert sonatas for him. Karl Stern was, indeed, a skilled pianist and his repertoire went far beyond the works of Franz Schubert. When Stern, himself, needed psychiatric attention, Pieper, serving as his mentor, was happy to accept Stern's renditions of Beethoven sonatas as payment. He was also very knowledgeable about music in general and could hold his own in esoteric conversations about the finer points of music with world class musicians such as Rudolf Serkin.

In his book *The Hand of God*,[6] Bernard Nathanson, who studied medicine under Stern, refers to him as the one

---

[6]   B. N. Nathanson, *The Hand of God: A Journey from Death to Life by The Abortion Doctor Who Changed His Mind* (Washington, DC: Regnery Publishing, (2013).

professor who made the greatest impression on him. He identified his former teacher as "a profoundly erudite psychiatrist who was, in the McGill [Montreal] professional galaxy, a star among stars." He admitted owing more to Stern than he initially realized.

His biographer, Daniel Burston, interviewed people who remembered Karl Stern as a novelist. Others saw him as a psychoanalyst for priests. He was also a neurologist and a gifted writer. Who is Karl Stern (1906–1975)? Is he the same person who is a pianist, musicologist, psychiatrist, neurologist, novelist, teacher, and writer? He was all these, in addition to being a husband and father. He was, perhaps, as some have said, the last Renaissance man.

Karl Stern was born in a small town in Bavaria to socially assimilated Jewish parents. When he was a teenager, he attended a Jewish synagogue, but soon became an atheist Zionist. He studied medicine at the Universities of Berlin, Munich, and Frankfort, before finding work in neurological research in England, and later as a lecturer in neuropathology at the Montreal Neurological Institute under Wilder Penfield.

Two of his books, *The Third Revolution* (1954)[7] and *The Flight from Woman* (1965),[8] are clearly masterpieces illustrating his keen insights into both culture and philosophy. They are even more relevant today than when they were written. The former centers on three great intellectual revolutions that

---

[7]   K. Stern, *The Third Revolution: Psychiatry and Religion* (New York: Harcourt, Brace, 1954).

[8]   Karl Stern, *The Flight from Woman*, (New York: Farrar, Straus and Giroux, 1965).

have taken place in the modern world involving, respectively, Marx, Darwin, and Freud. Each represents the concomitant reduction of reality to matter and the dehumanization of man. The first was Karl Marx's economic revolution whose dialectical materialism led directly to atheistic communism. Secondly, the biological revolution introduced by Charles Darwin led to the racist theory of Nazi Germany. Finally, Sigmund Freud inaugurated a psychological revolution that has threatened man's spirituality. Stern exposes the error of reducing various levels of reality to matter and how it has an adverse effect on man. At the same time, Stern explains, as St. Thomas did, how religion and science, faith and reason, are harmonious with each other.

Stern is particularly adept in debunking the "nothing but" philosophies of Marx and Freud: "If Marx, instead of saying, 'Religion is nothing but the opiate of the people,'" said, "Woe unto you who use religion as an opiate of the people," he would have been on firm ground. Had Freud told his patients, "'What you call religion is actually your neurosis,' instead of claiming that religion is actually your neurosis, he would have stated a frequently observed truth."

The Flight from Woman is a study of the polarity between the sexes. As a psychiatrist, Stern draws attention to the problem of activism, a lack of balance between action and contemplation. Underlying this problem, which is found more extensively in men, is a maternal conflict and a rejection of the feminine. Technological society is not congenial to tempering an excessively rational approach to life: "an undue emphasis on the technical and the rational, and a rejection of what for want of a better term we call 'feeling,' go hand in hand with a neurotic dread of receiving a fear of tenderness and of protection—and are invariably associated with an original maternal conflict." Rationalism and positivism have influenced the modern world over the last three centuries to an extraordinary degree. The result has been a flight from the feminine, from feeling, from the tenderness of the human heart.

But *The Pillar of Fire*[9] was, far and away, Karl Stern's best-seller. It is regarded by many reviewers as the most outstanding account of a personal conversion from Judaism to Catholicism of the twentieth century. Bernard Nathanson, who made the same conversion, tells us that "with each reading" of Stern's extended letter to his brother, which constitutes the final chapter of the book, "I found myself fighting back the tears."

Stern's conversion story is by no means a solitary adventure. Along the way, Stern met or corresponded with C. S. Lewis, Dorothy Day, Jacques Maritain, Gabriel Marcel, Claire Booth Luce, Graham Greene, Reinhold Niebuhr, Thomas Merton, Robert Lowell, and many others. In a private conversation with Maritain, Karl Stern, psychiatrist that he was, confessed a concern that his conversion might be nothing but a mirage rooted in an unconscious desire to escape the destiny of a Jew. Maritain's response reads like a page from *The Third Revolution*. He warned Stern against allowing his spiritual experiences to be corroded by psychological analysis. The genuineness of Stern's spiritual experiences, said Maritain, "occur on a plane quite apart from

---

9   Karl Stern, *The Pillar of Fire* (New York: Harcourt, 1951).

that of primitive emotions." Years later, Stern would write, in *The Third Revolution,* "If someone comes to believe that the Freudian concepts are all there is to the nature of Man, he loses sight of the ultimate design."

Stern remained true to that ultimate design. At the close of *The Pillar of Fire,* he states, like the narrator in Francis Thompson's "The Hound of Heaven," that there was no doubt about the fact that with regard to the course of his life "towards Him we had been running, or from Him we had been running away, but all the time He had been in the center of things."

Wanda Poltawska

The city was Toledo, Ohio. The year was 1990. The venue was the dining room in a private home. The audience consisted of several pro-life people, including myself. The speaker was Wanda Poltawska who was relating a series of events in her life that we were most privileged to hear.

In 1962, doctors, after diagnosing Poltawska as having throat cancer, planned to subject her to a desperate medical procedure. The auxiliary bishop of Cracow, Karol Wojtyla, a close friend of Wanda, and being vitally concerned about her condition, dispatched a letter to Padre Pio, requesting his intervention: "Venerable Father, I ask that you pray for a forty-year-old mother of four girls, in Cracow, Poland (who during the last war spent five years in a concentration camp), who is now in very grave danger related to her health and possibly may die of cancer: that God may extend his mercy to this woman and her family in the presence of the Most Blessed Virgin. Most obligated in Christ, Karol Wojtyla."

Angelo Battisti, the administrator of the House for the

Relief of Suffering, a hospital which Padre Pio helped to build, offers the following personal testimony: "Having just arrived at the monastery, Padre Pio told me to read the letter to him. He listened to the brief message in Latin, then said: 'To this request one cannot say "no,"' and then added, 'Angelino, save this letter because one day it will become important.'" The saint's directive was prophetic. The letter was included in the canonization process for Saint John Paul II.

The hoped-for miracle occurred. Just before the scheduled surgical procedure, Wanda Poltawska's health was completely restored. However, owing to her scientific temperament (she was a trained psychiatrist), Dr. Poltawska was hesitant to believe that she was the recipient of a miracle. Therefore, she traveled to Pietrelcina, where the Capuchin friar resided. Not knowing where to find Padre Pio, she found herself standing outside of a church asking a passerby where he might be. She was then told that she was standing outside of the very church where Padre Pio was saying Mass. Dr. Poltawska entered the church. During the celebration of the Mass, the now canonized saint paused momentarily and looked directly at the pilgrim from Poland, conveying to her the assurance that he knew that she was the woman for whom he had prayed.

This was a series of events that Wanda was only too happy to relate. Her internment in the Ravensbrück concentration camp for nearly five years was quite another matter.

In September of 1939, the Nazis invaded Poland. Their aim was to subjugate the Polish people, whom they did not regard as exactly human beings, according to their Arian ideology. "Re-education" (a word that was a euphemism for dehumanization) was needed. Any resistance on the part of Poles was severely punished, usually by internment or death. Wanda Poltawska was arrested for the crime of carrying letters and orders to various Resistance groups. She was beaten badly and ultimately sent to the Ravensbrück camp where she remained for nearly five years. There, she was subjected to horrific psychological humiliations and physical injuries. She was used as a "guinea pig." Diseased bacilli was injected into her bone marrow, for no other reason than to find out how the body might react to this disease. She managed to survive whereas many died or were executed.

When she returned home in the spring of 1945, she was tormented by "frighteningly realistic" nightmares about the camp to the extent that she dared not sleep. By contrast, while she was at Ravensbrück, she dreamed of the comforts of home. A psychiatrist advised her to write out her horrors as a way of exorcising them. The advice worked, though she did not want to share her experiences with anyone else. Consequently, *And I Am Afraid of My Dreams*[10] remained in a drawer for fifteen years until she was finally persuaded to publish it. Mary Craig, who translated the book into English, states that it gives "a priceless insight into a dark period of human history which we might prefer to forget, but which it might be wiser to try to understand."

"Hunger is a terrible thing," she writes, though it was not the most horrible thing she experienced in the camp. It is "monstrous and indescribable." Yet something inside Wanda

---

[10]   Wanda Półtawska and Mary Craig, *And I Am Afraid of My Dreams* (New York: Hippocrene, 2012).

Poltawska—her will to live, her pledge to become a doctor, her sense of herself as a human being,—kept her going: "I must, simply *must* get the better of my hungry body. I *will* not stop being myself just because I am hungry." She knew, decisively, that she was far more than "prisoner number 7709." "I never lost that interior freedom," she tells her readers. Tragically, ninety-two thousand women and children perished in the unimaginably inhuman conditions of Ravensbrück.

Wanda Poltawska went on to become a psychiatrist, specializing in the treatment of juvenile patients, including the deeply-traumatized "Auschwitz children" who had been born or incarcerated in the Nazi concentration camps. She worked in the psychiatric clinic of Cracow's Jagiellonian University. In addition, she was appointed by Pope John II as Director of the Marriage and Family Institute in Cracow, Poland, and became an important advisor to the pontiff on matters of marriage and the family. Both she and her philosopher husband, Andrzej, were appointed members of the Papal Commission on Family Matters.

After reading *And I Am Afraid of My Dreams*, one reviewer made the comment that he is now able to read the personalism of John Paul II "in a new and dramatic way." Dr. Poltawska's life includes the best and the worst of the twentieth century. It is testimony to the best inasmuch as it reveals the strength of the person, the capacity to transcend evil, and the insistence of living in accord with one's dignity as a human being. Wanda Poltawska has shown us that one's sense of inner dignity can prevail under conditions of the utmost barbarity. She demonstrates for all of us both the grittiness of human existence and the value of life.

Herbert Ratner

Herbert Ratner was the youngest of seven children, born on May 23, 1907 in New York City to Jewish-Russian immigrants. His father, a socialist who had no use for religion, named him after the English philosopher Herbert Spencer who is best remembered for his expression, "the survival of the fittest." He would have been prescient had he named his son Thomas, after Saint Thomas Aquinas. Sometimes the apple does fall far from the tree.

Herbert did inherit from his father a love for medicine and earned his MD from the University of Michigan in 1935. While in Ann Arbor, he met and subsequently married Dorothy Smith, a fellow medical student and the daughter of a farm family of twelve children. From 1934 to 1936, Herb and Dorothy were research assistants at the University of Michigan. Herb studied public health and, in his off hours, took courses in philosophy. The harmonious interface between medicine and philosophy was to be a life-long preoccupation for him.

In 1937, Robert Maynard Hutchins, president of the University of Chicago, appointed Dr. Ratner as senior member of the Committee of Liberal Arts. There, he did research on the history of medicine as an assistant to Mortimer Adler, the founder of the Great Books Program. Adler, who was a Thomist, spearheaded a re-examination of the classical thinkers, particularly Aristotle and Aquinas. Impressed with the philosophy of Aquinas, many became attracted to the Catholic Church. In 1938, Herb converted to Catholicism and remained a faithful and devoted member of the Church throughout his life. He was a long-time and active member of the Chicago Catholic Physicians Guild and served as president of the Catholic Medical Association.

Having studied Aristotle and Aquinas, he realized all the more clearly the essential role of nature not only for medicine but also for the family. In an article entitled "The Family: Nature's Institution," he paid homage to what the great Thomist and historian of philosophy Etienne Gilson said of St. Thomas's thinking: "The central intuition which governs the whole philosophical and theological undertaking of Saint Thomas is that it is impossible to do justice to God without doing justice to nature, and that doing justice to nature is at the same time the surest way of doing justice to God."

Thus, Nature was a "Vicar General." And just as the vicar is of one mind with his superior, so, too, nature has a similar relationship with her Creator. In an address to members of the Fellowship of Catholic Scholars in 1988, Dr. Ratner told his audience that "the notion of nature as a Vicar General is a realistic and dynamic concept of nature which recognizes man as an integral part of biological nature and the universe 'tied within the divine mind by an indissoluble knot.'" With regard to the family, he stated, "The battle for the survival of the family centers in good part around the explication of the family as a natural institution communicating nature's wisdom with its inherent power to persuade human reason and free choice."

It was inevitable, therefore, that Dr. Ratner would have much to say about the natural benefits of breastfeeding. His most treasured quotation on the naturalness of breast-feeding is borrowed from the jurist Oliver Wendell Homes: "A pair of mammary glands are more advantageous in the art of compounding a nutritive fluid for infants than the two hemispheres of the most learned professor's brain." For Ratner, the appropriate gifts that nature has bestowed on the mother cannot be stressed enough. Nature endows the mother with smooth skin, a soprano voice, cradle arms, and the intuitive ability to understand the natural language of infant facial expressions. Ratner was a senior advisor to the La Leche League from its inception and for more than forty years.

In his tribute to Dr. Ratner, his long-time friend and associate Dr. Eugene Diamond affirmed that Herb "was that rarest of personalities, a true intellectual who was at the same time warm, approachable and witty." The latter virtue predominated on many occasions. I recall being on a bus with him while he was entertaining everyone with one-liners: "Have you heard about the romance between the Tower of London and the Leaning Tower of Pisa? He had the time and she had the inclination." Then, I would hear him say, in

Henny Youngman-like fashion, "I'm not getting a laugh; can you all hear me?"

I found him to be most approachable. He was delighted when I mentioned to him that "nature is the home team and the home team bats last," and used it (even crediting me) in subsequent presentations. He was editor of *Child and Family Quarterly* for twenty-nine years and invited me to serve on the editorial board. The quarterly had broad influence and dealt with a range of topics including breastfeeding, nutrition, preventative medicine, AIDS, the side-effects of contraception, the value of children, and the evils of abortion. A regular feature, dear to his heart, was "Recent setbacks in medicine." An avid historian, Ratner would reprint such out-of-the-way articles as seventeenth-century theologian Jeremy Taylor's "The Duty of Nursing Your Child in Imitation of the Blessed Mother."

Ratner was always swimming against the popular tide, though his thinking was always well-grounded in nature and good medicine. Critical of how careless Americans were about their health, and more concerned with stating the facts than playing the game, he claimed that "America is the most over-medicated, most over-operated, and most over-inoculated country in the world. . . . We are flabby and overweight. . . . We can't sleep; we can't get going when we are awake." After serving as public health physician for Oak Park, Illinois, he was dismissed, as he explained to me, because he was pro-life.

In 1985, the "Fellowship of Catholic Scholars presented Dr. Ratner with the Cardinal Wright Award for embodying the fellowship's goal of integrating learning and religious faith. At that time, Ratner reiterated that he had dedicated his long career to promoting traditional family values and to the proposition that "children are a gift of nature and a blessing from God."

Dr. Herbert Ratner passed away on December 6, 1997, while visiting his daughter in Cleveland, at the age of ninety. We pray that his legacy will endure.

THE BLESSINGS AND CHALLENGES OF LIFE

Eugene Diamond

In the final scene of Thornton Wilder's play *Our Town,* Emily is granted a special privilege. She is allowed to return from the grave to Grover's Corners, New Hampshire and re-experience any particular day of her choosing. She selects her twelfth birthday. Emily agonizes over the recapitulation of this day since she now realizes that every moment of life should be treasured. "It goes so fast," she exclaims, "we don't have time to look at one another! Do any human beings ever realize life while they live it—every, every minute?" "No," replies the Stage Manager. "The saints and poets maybe—they do some."

One might add to "saints and poets," *lovers.* In a letter to his wife early in their marriage, Eugene Diamond recalled their courtship period when their relationship advanced from "the hollow safety of banter to the stage where pilgrim souls communicated and each somehow knew that there had been a discovery. What had been discovered was the rest of one's self." Eugene and Rosemary were married. The first two pregnancies ended in miscarriages. Then followed thirteen healthy children, seven sons and six daughters, all of whom advanced to graduate education, four of them becoming physicians. A photo adorns the cover of Dr. Diamond's book *The Large Family: A Blessing and a Challenge*,[11] showing mom and dad surrounded by their children, in-laws and grandchildren, all fifty-eight of them. One reviewer declared, "And you never saw such a lineup of beautiful girls, handsome young men and lovely children. What an achievement! Diamonds are forever!"

I was a guest at the Diamond's home in suburban Chicago. Life in a large household can be complicated. One of the children inadvertently drove off with my luggage. Gene and Rosemary took me to a restaurant in Chicago where we were entertained by a performance, in a distinctively Italian accent, of "I'm a Rhina Stona Cowboy."

Dr. Diamond has enjoyed a distinguished career as a pediatrician as professor of Pediatrics and past chairman of the Department of Pediatrics at Loyola University Stritch School of Medicine. He was visiting professor at Rush Medical College from 1967–69 and a member of numerous medical associations. He held presidential positions at the Catholic Physician's Guild, Illinois Academy of Pediatrics, World Federation of Doctors Who Respect Life, Calumet Physician's Guilds, and other medical organizations.

Dr. Diamond received his MD from Loyola University and his pediatric training from the University of Chicago. He

---

[11]   Eugene F. Diamond *The Large Family: A Blessing and a Challenge* (San Francisco: Ignatius Press, 1996).

is the recipient of a number of prestigious awards including Pediatrician of the Year-Illinois Chapter, American Academy of Pediatrics, in 1980; the George Award in Clinical Pediatrics in 1981; and the Summerhill Award from Birthright International in 1995. An accomplished writer, Dr. Diamond has published several books, including a novel. He served as editor-in-chief and executive editor of *The Linacre Quarterly* and was president of the Catholic Medical Association from 1979–80.

Eugene F. Diamond was born in Chicago in 1932 during the very worst time of the Depression. His father died when he was six years old. As a consequence, he was brought up in poverty. He entered the US Navy at seventeen and eventually qualified for the GI Bill, which paid for his medical education. As a doctor, he was involved in a multitude of activities ranging from various pediatric responsibilities to sports medicine and bioethical concerns. He became a close friend of Dr. Herbert Ratner, who served as his mentor until the latter's death in 1997. He credits Ratner for helping him to think about moral issues and lauded him as a "great Socratic teacher."

Apart from his family and medical practice, Diamond also distinguished himself in the field of law. An Illinois law had been passed granting parents the right to notification if a child (an unmarried minor) of theirs was about to have an abortion. It passed both houses but was vetoed by Governor James Thompson. Nonetheless, it was passed over his veto, a clear indication that the law reflected the will of the people. Parents wanted to be notified if their minor child was seeking an abortion. Nonetheless, the American Civil Liberties

Union challenged the law and the case went before a federal justice. When a district court found the law to be unconstitutional, Dr. Diamond, on the basis of his conscientious objection to abortions, his status as a pediatrician, and as a parent of a minor daughter, filed a motion to intervene as a defendant of the law. The US Supreme Court, in *Diamond v. Charles*, upheld the "unconstitutionality" of the law in 1986. The court argued that the notification provision "is not to be placed in the hands of 'concerned bystanders,' who will use it simply as a 'vehicle for the vindication of value interests.'"

Diamond was chastised for being "capricious" in defending the notification right. "Well," Diamond would later state, reflecting on actions of the courts, "how can I be capricious when I am representing a law that was overwhelmingly passed? But this is the kind treatment that you sometimes get in the courts, that just absolutely boggles your mind. I was in the middle of trying to get kids through college and pay their tuition, and suddenly I get assessed $250,000." In a statement which is a model of understatement, Diamond claimed that "we're not getting a fair shake."

Writing for the *National Catholic Bioethics Quarterly* (Summer 2013), Dr. Diamond conveyed serious concerns about the consequences of the Patient Protection Care Act of 2010. He expressed his dismay that advisors to President Obama demonstrated an overriding concern for cost over care. He was also critical of subtle encouragement of physician-assisted suicide in hospices and long-term-care facilities. At the same time, he argued that modern advances in medicine have made pain control an achievable right. "Recognizing the right of patients who are terminally ill to obtain effective pain control," he wrote, "is an important factor in the opposition to health care rationing and euthanasia."

Eugene Diamond was always a champion for the sick, the neglected, and the marginalized. His faith in God, together with the strength of his family, was his powerhouse. Without that strength it is hard to understand how any person could continue to give so much while being opposed so vehemently. "Character is formed in the stormy billows of the world," wrote Johann Wolfgang von Goethe. That is the challenge. But it is also formed in the warmth of a loving family. That is the blessing.

A Man of Graciousness

Walker Percy

When Ted Williams homered in his last at bat and did not tip his cap to the cheering crowd, novelist John Updike, who was present at the game, remarked that "Gods don't answer letters." If we can deify the Splendid Splinter, we can also deify Walker Percy who has proven that the Gods sometimes *do* answer letters. Percy took the time to send me a handwritten letter thanking me for sending him a copy of my review of his *Lost in the Cosmos: The Last Self-Help Book*. It was most gracious of him to do so.

The *New York Times*, though it found *Lost in the Cosmos* "charming, whimsical, slyly profound," saw fit not to answer the best-selling novelist's letter concerning the controversial issue of abortion. On January 22, 1988, the fifteenth anniversary of *Roe v. Wade*, Percy dispatched a letter to the esteemed newspaper warning that "once the principle [of "getting rid of the unwanted"] gains acceptance—juridically, medically, socially—innocent human life can be destroyed for whatever reason—then it does not take a prophet to predict what will happen next." Percy wrote to the *Times* once again, on February 15, to ascertain whether his initial letter was received. Again, Dr. Percy received no reply. Walker Percy, then, is both a witness to life and also a witness to the false claim that the *New York Times* is a liberal organ that is unwilling to suppress dissent.

Graciousness is a marvelous virtue. It does not allow class distinctions or any other kind of distinction to prevent a person from seeing the worth of others. The Apostle of Life is a person of graciousness. Percy was certainly gracious to the unborn child, recognizing him as a *bona fide* member of the human family. It is a fact, he wrote, "known to every high-school student . . . that the life of every individual organism, human or not, begins when the chromosomes of the sperm fuse with the chromosomes of the ovum to form a new DNA complex that henceforth directs the ontogenesis of the organism." The irony here, for Percy, is that the beginning of life is not a religious dogma but a fact of science. Those who advocate for abortion suppress a scientific fact whereas defenders of life honor it. With this in mind, Percy offers a scenario in which the Supreme Court cross-examines a high-school biology teacher and admonishes him that it is only his personal opinion that the fertilized egg is the beginning of life. The teacher is enjoined never to impose his private beliefs on his students. "Like Galileo," writes Percy, "he caves in, submits, but in turning away is heard to murmur, *"But it's still alive!"*

Walker Percy's life reads like a Russian novel. His grandfather committed suicide in 1917, the year after Walker was born. Then came the double tragedy of his father's suicide and his mother's apparent suicide one year later in an automobile accident. He was adopted at the age of fourteen, along with his two brothers, by William Alexander Percy, a cousin once removed. "Uncle Will" introduced his nephew to Brahms, Shakespeare, and Keats. Nonetheless, Percy's education up to the age of thirty was almost exclusively scientific. He received his medical degree with highest honors from Columbia University. While interning at New York's Bellevue Hospital, he performed many autopsies on indigent alcoholics, some of whom died of tuberculosis. He contracted the highly contagious disease and was sent to a sanatorium in upstate New York for two years of convalescence. He returned to his active life as an instructor of pathology at Columbia medical school. Within a few months, however, he suffered a relapse and was sent to a home in Connecticut where, it is said, he occupied the same bed formerly used by four-time Pulitzer Prize winning playwright Eugene O'Neill.

Percy used his enforced passivity as an active instrument. He read Aquinas, Dostoevsky, Maritain, Marcel, Kierkegaard, Tolstoy, and Camus. He began writing philosophical articles. "If the first great intellectual discovery of my life was the beauty of the scientific method," he wrote, "surely the second was the discovery of the singular predicament of man in the very world which has been transformed by science."

Dr. Percy, who was then forty-four years old, strongly identified with the Russian playwright Anton Chekhov; like Percy, Chekhov could no longer practice medicine because of his tubercular condition and turned to writing. Chekhov died at age forty-four. Walker Percy had a long road ahead of him.

Not long after his release from the Connecticut sanatorium, he married Mary Bernice Townsend, a medical technician. Six month later, after studying Catholicism together, he and his wife, on November 7, 1947, entered the Catholic Church. Unable to practice medicine because of his weakened condition, he turned to writing. His first novel, *The Moviegoer*,[12] after extensive revisions, won the coveted National Book Award. Five novels, all best-sellers, followed, establishing him as one of the most important literary figures on the American scene. In one of the foremost works about Percy—*Walker Percy: an American Search*[13]—Robert Coles praised him for having "a sharp eye for all the pompous self-important and self-centered baloney that is eating away at American secular culture—its moral drift, its egoism, rootlessness and greed" and for being "onto both the liberals and the conservatives" and hitting "the blind spots in both camps." Dr. Walker Percy the trained pathologist, was applying his diagnostic skills to a moribund culture.

Walker Percy passed away in May of 1990 of prostate cancer eighteen days before his seventy-fourth birthday. He is buried on the grounds of St. Joseph Benedictine Abbey in St. Benedict, Louisiana. He had become a secular oblate of the abbey's monastic community and had made his final oblation on February 16, 1990. On occasion of his death, Cleanth Brooks, literary critic and Yale University professor,

---

12   Walker Percy, *The Moviegoer* (New York: Alfred A. Knopf, 1961).
13   Robert Coles, *Walker Percy: An American Search* (Boston, Mass: Little, Brown, 1979).

wrote, "In losing Walker Percy, we have lost a remarkable figure in American literature, and a generous man. Some of us have lost a kind and dear friend." The latter encomium is affirmed by many.

PART II

Apostles From the World of Philosophy

Dietrich von Hildebrand

A lice von Hildebrand titled the biography of her husband *The Soul of a Lion* (2000). In the foreword to the book, chronicling the life of one of the twentieth century's greatest Catholic philosophers, Cardinal Ratzinger (later Pope Benedict XVI) refers to an "epiphanous" moment when Dietrich von Hildebrand first realized the nature and importance of philosophy. He describes what transpired during the course of a long walk with one of his sisters when the young Dietrich persistently rebuffed her protestations that moral values are relative. He answered each of her propositions vigorously with a counter argument of his own. Exasperated, the sister called upon their father for assistance. "Imagine, Father," the distraught sibling complained, "Dietrich refuses to acknowledge that all moral values are relative." "Do not forget," the father responded, "that he is only fourteen." Infuriated by his father's curt remark, the boy answered, "Father, if you have no better argument than my age to offer against my position, then your own position must rest on very shaky grounds."

Dietrich grew into manhood without ever losing his conviction that moral values cannot be relative. His love for truth led him into the Catholic Church when he was twenty-four. It also earned him the nickname, "Knight of Truth." His love for the Church led him to guide many of his family members into the Church. All five of his sisters became Catholic, and his influence on four of them was decisive.

When people have wildly conflicting notions about what is and what is not moral, the situation is ripe for someone to come along and re-establish order. A society cannot function cohesively when there is moral chaos. And relativism in practice is, indeed, society in chaos. As history has shown, unbridled moral conflict has often led people to escape from their "freedom" into the arms of tyranny.

Dietrich Richard Alfred von Hildebrand was born in Florence, Italy on October 12, 1889 (the same day as Christopher Dawson) amidst the artistic splendor of that great city. His father was a renowned sculptor whom the King of Bavaria knighted in 1904. To the Hildebrand household came a steady stream of outstanding artists and thinkers, including Richard and Cosima Wagner, Franz Liszt, Richard Strauss, Henty James, Rudolf Otto, Rainer Maria Rilke, Wilhelm Furtwängler, and British Prime Minister William Gladstone. Out of this highly cultured milieu was formed, in the heart and soul of the young von Hildebrand, a profound love of beauty and a deep regard for reverence, values that he wrote about extensively in his many works on ethics and aesthetics.

At age forty-five, the man who refused to believe that moral values are relative had the singular honor of being called "enemy number one" of National Socialism by the German ambassador in Vienna, Franz von Papen. It was only through Divine Providence, together with the help of many courageous and generous friends, that von Hildebrand avoided capture and execution (an order had been issued for his assassination) and escaped in 1940 to America where he began a distinguished career at Fordham University as a teacher, and subsequently became world renowned as a writer and lecturer.

A Knight for Truth set out in a relativistic world may seem quixotic. No doubt it seems exactly that to the secular world where political correctness is enshrined as a *summum bonum*. Relativism is *au courant*. It appears to be broad-minded, tolerant, and democratic. But it is essentially unrealistic, and consequently unworkable. Only truth can be the unifying basis for a civil society. Radical disagreement on moral issues (abortion, euthanasia, same-sex marriage, etc.) invites a Leviathan of state control.

The truth of the human being is that he is a creature who is called to love, work for peace, and enjoy (if not create) things of beauty. That is what Dietrich von Hildebrand understood and that was what constituted the vision to which he dedicated his entire life. In his writing he avoided extravagant speculations. His concern was primarily with the seemingly "everyday" experiences of human beings. Hence, he wrote extensively about the interior and ethical life of the human person and his obligations to others. Because his Catholic faith imbued his thinking, he is known, alongside of such stalwarts as Saint John Paul II, Jacques Maritain, Gabriel Marcel, Emmanuel Mourier, as a Christian personalist.

Of his more than thirty published books, among the most important are: *In Defense of Purity* (1935), *Liturgy and Personality* (1943), *Transformation in Christ* (1948), *The New Tower of Babel* (1953), and *The Trojan Horse in the City of God* (1967).[14]

Pope Pius XII referred to von Hildebrand as "a 20th Century doctor of the Church." When Pope Paul VI published *Humane Vitae* in 1968, von Hildebrand was one of the first Catholic thinkers to defend it publicly. Saint John Paul II acknowledged his own intellectual debt to him, especially on the subject of marriage. And, as Pope Benedict XVI has remarked, "I am personally convinced that, when, at some time in the future, the intellectual history of the Catholic Church in the twentieth century is written, the name Dietrich von Hildebrand will be most prominent among the figures of our time."

In recent years there has been a resurgence of interest in the thought of von Hildebrand. Partly responsible for this resurgence is the work of "The Dietrich von Hildebrand Legacy Project" established in 2004. The purpose of the project is not only to translate and publish certain writings of von

---

14   Dietrich Von Hildebrand, *In Defense of Purity: An Analysis of the Catholic Ideals of Purity and Virginity* (New York: Sheed and Ward, 1935); *Liturgy and Personality: The Healing Power of Formal Prayer* (Manchester, NH: Sophia Institute Press, 1993); *Transformation in Christ* (Franciscan Herald Press, 1948); *The New Tower of Babel: Essays* (London: Burns & Oates, 1953); *Trojan Horse in the City of God* (Chicago: Franciscan Herald, 1967).

Hildebrand into English, but to facilitate the reception of his works by a larger audience. To this end, a conference in Rome was held in May 2010—"The Christian Personalism of Dietrich von Hildebrand"—featuring the critical reception of his book *The Nature of Love*,[15] published for the first time in English in 2009.

In 1977, when he was close to death, he spoke to his wife in his native tongue. His voice had become a whisper, but his wife could hear him say, "I used to be a lion; now I am but a helpless little thing." He then took a deep breath and added, "*Ma sai, sai, la mia anima è ancora un leone* ("But you know, you know, my soul is still a lion"). Her husband's very last words, according to her account, uttered with a trembling voice, were, "A country that legalizes murder is doomed."

---

[15]   Dietrich Von Hildebrand, John F. Crosby, John Henry Crosby, and Kenneth L. Schmitz, *The Nature of Love*, (2009).

Mortimer Adler

When he was lecturing at the University of Chicago, Mortimer Adler identified himself as a Jew teaching Catholic philosophy at a Protestant school to a class of atheists. The image of not quite fitting in was characteristic of Adler's life, though he was never one to complain about it. The absence of any rough edges has never been a formula for the development of personal authenticity. The unobstructed life, a modern Socrates might say, is not worth living perhaps even less than the unexamined life.

Mortimer Jerome Adler was born in New York City in the year 1902 to Jewish immigrants. His early ambition was to become a journalist which led him to drop out of school at the tender age of fourteen to serve as a copy boy for the *New York Sun*. His hiatus from formal education, however, was short-lived. Reading the great thinkers at night inspired him to enroll at Columbia University where he excelled but did not graduate. He refused to take the required swimming test in order to earn his bachelor's degree. The school later apologized for this peculiarity and awarded him an honorary degree in 1983.

Robert Hutchins, who had befriended Adler, appointed him professor of the philosophy of law at the University of Chicago in 1930. The appointment was met with opposition from several faculty members who entertained grave doubts about his competence as a non-lawyer teaching in a law school.

Adler and Hutchins went on to found the Great Books of the western world program and the Great Books Foundation. This, too, was greeted with strong criticism. One fellow academic claimed that the Great Books showed a "profound disrespect for the intellectual capacities of color—red, brown or yellow." Adler, however, was more interested in great ideas than in politics. He insisted that ethnic quotas were irrelevant to his project. He placed no limitations on his readers, however. "Philosophy is everybody's business," he maintained. Another critic remarked that it seemed to him that the Great Books "were an excellent instrument for perpetuating errors." Adler was well aware of the philosophical errors of the great writers, but he wanted people to familiarize themselves with the great ideas—such as love, justice, beauty, goodness, truth, and God—and discuss them thoroughly. The Great Books was merely a launching pad.

Criticisms of Dr. Adler's popularizing efforts invited scorn that bordered on the humorous. One critic called him "the Charles Atlas of Western intellection," and another dismissed him as "the Lawrence Welk of the philosophy trade." Some denigrated him as a lightweight, while others regarded him as something of a crank. Adler always held his ground.

It was not that he was stubborn. He was thoughtful and had the courage to remain firm in his convictions. Moreover, his scholarship could not be questioned. To take but one example, he and his colleagues at the Institute for Philosophical Research spent ten years studying the notion of freedom prior to Adler's publication of *The Idea of Freedom: A Dialectical Examination of the Conceptions of Freedom.*[16]

Adler discovered St. Thomas Aquinas in his early twenties. What he admired about Thomas was the "intellectual austerity, integrity, precision and brilliance" he found in the Angelic Doctor's writings. As a result, he put the study of theology highest among all his philosophical interests. Though not a Christian, Adler spoke frequently at Catholic institutions and was a regular contributor to Catholic journals. Nonetheless, his adoption of St. Thomas placed him outside of the mainstream of professional philosophers.

An additional beef that his colleagues raised against him was that he wrote for the masses. "Unlike many of my contemporaries," he once stated, "I never write books for my fellow professors to read. I have no interest in the academic audience at all. I'm interested in Joe Doakes. A general audience can read any book I write—and they do." He regarded academic jargon, esoteric language, and footnotes to be obstacles for his readers. His critics may have been more motivated by envy than argumentation since many of Adler's books, including *How to Read a Book,* were

---

[16]   Mortimer Jerome Adler, *The Idea of Freedom* (Garden City, NY: Doubleday, 1958).

best-sellers. Concerning that work, one acid-penned critic urged Adler to read *How to Write a Book*.[17]

On a personal note, when I presented my dog-eared copy of that work to Dr. Adler, he expressed his pleasure that my tattered copy was proof that it had been well-read. I have often used, in my classroom presentations, his simple but effective way of distinguishing between true liberalism and false liberalism: "The liberal who frees himself *from* reason, rather than *through* it, surrenders to the only other arbiter in human affairs—force, or what Mr. Chamberlain has called 'the awful arbitrament of war.'" Would that our present society could grasp and take to heart the illuminating significance of that single sentence!

Adler authored fifty or so books and established himself as America's premier educator and philosopher. He was a man of outstanding intellectual gifts. At the same time, he understood the value of not thinking. "In idling," he once remarked, "the motor's running, but your mind takes in anything. Things pop into it. Those are the gifts of subterranean conscious."

Often resisted in his life and yet always yearning to fit in, Adler, who was eminently Catholic in mind, delayed entering the Church until his wife, an Episcopalian, passed away in 1998. According to one of his colleagues, Adler "had been attracted to Catholicism for many years" and "wanted to be a Roman Catholic, but issues like abortion and the resistance of his family and friends" kept him away.

---

[17]   Mortimer Jerome Adler, *How to Read a Book: A Guide to Reading the Great Books* (New York: Simon and Schuster, 1966).

In December 1999, however, Mortimer Adler was formally received into the Catholic Church. His long-time friend Bishop Pierre DuMaine officiated. "Finally," wrote another friend, Professor Ralph McInerny, "he became the Roman Catholic he had been training to be all his life." Finally, we might add, he fit in without either resistance or rough edges. At the time of his passing, he was survived by four sons, six grandchildren, and two great-grandchildren. His contribution to life may have outweighed his contribution to knowledge.

Saint Thomas Aquinas

Thomas Aquinas was born in the year 1224 in Rocca Sicca, the hereditary castle of the counts of Aquino in the Neapolitan province. While he was residing in the womb, a holy man brought a prophecy to the unborn child's mother, Theodora, Countess of Aquino: "Rejoice, O lady, for thou art about to have a son whom thou shalt call Thomas. . . . Such will be his learning and holiness that his equal will not be found throughout the world."

The prophecy was fulfilled. At the hearing for the canonization of Saint Thomas Aquinas in 1319, a statement from the archbishop of Naples was introduced. According to the testimony of the good bishop, Friar Giacomo di Viterbo, "Our savior had sent, as doctor of truth to illuminate the world and the universal Church, first the apostle Paul, then Augustine, and finally in these latest days Friar Thomas, whom . . . no one would succeed till the end of the world."

This testimony properly recognizes Saint Thomas Aquinas's rightful place as a pre-eminent Doctor of the Church.

This most distinguished honor was ratified by Pope Leo XIII in his encyclical *Aeterni Patris*: "Let carefully selected teachers endeavor to implant the doctrine of Thomas Aquinas in the minds of students, and set forth clearly his solidity and excellence over others. Let the universities already founded or to be founded by you [venerable brethren] illustrate and defend this doctrine, and use it for the refutation of prevailing errors."

Other popes have lavished similar praise upon the Angelic Doctor. In his encyclical *Humani Generis*, Pope Pius XII declared, "Since, as we well know from the experience of centuries, the method of Aquinas is singularly preeminent both for teaching students and for bringing truth to light; his doctrine is in harmony with divine revelation, and is most effective both for safeguarding the foundation of faith, and for reaping, safely and useful, the fruits of sound progress."

It is important to note that Aquinas is not great because the Church states that he is great; rather the Church recognizes the greatness that is demonstrated in Aquinas's writings. Jacques Maritain, the twentieth century's foremost Thomistic philosopher, avers that Aquinas's philosophy is founded on evidence alone and continues to live by reason alone.

What is it that sets Aquinas apart from all the others? Peter Kreeft, in his summary of the *Summa Theologica*, states that Thomas Aquinas is the greatest of all philosophers because he is a beacon of "truth, common sense, practicality, clarity, profundity, orthodoxy, and modernity." A single sentence from his voluminous writings integrates all of these seven points: "The greatest kindness one can render to any man consists in leading him to truth." For Aquinas, truth can be known, communicated, and serve as a benefit for people. In clear and straightforward language, Aquinas states, "The truth of the human intellect receives its direction and measurement from the essences of things. For the truth or falsity of an opinion depends on whether a thing is or is not." In other words, the intellect makes contact with the external world and comes to know the truth of things as they are and not as one might have a subjective opinion of them. This is indeed practical because it is not at all practical for a person to reside in a dream world of private thoughts. Here, common sense, orthodoxy, and modernity come together. We emphasize "modernity" because such a sensible position holds true for all ages. Aquinas is modern, therefore, because his thought, not being restricted by what is fashionable, never goes out of style.

The distinguished Thomistic scholar Etienne Gilson has made the observation that Aquinas had two virtues to a very high degree that are seldom found as such in the same person. The virtues he specified are intellectual modesty and intellectual audacity. Aquinas was open to all thinkers and was astonishingly well read. Cardinal Cajetan said of him that because "he most venerated the ancient doctors of the Church, in a certain way seems to have inherited the intellect of all." Because of this intellectual modesty, Aquinas could understand what he read clearly and objectively without the intrusion of any personal bias. Because of his intellectual audacity, he had the strength of mind to hold on to what he understood without making any concessions to popular trends or to critics who had political power.

Therefore, Pope Leo XIII could say that "Thomas collected

together and cemented, distributed [the doctrines of his pre-decessors] in wonderful order, and so increased with important additions [the claim] that he is rightly and deservedly esteemed the special bulwark and glory of the Catholic faith." Aquinas saw clearly, held firmly, and ordered properly, both the truths of philosophy and those of revelation.

There are many philosophers who possessed intellectual modesty but lacked the audacity to hold on to what they knew and capitulated to political correctness. Among these thinkers can be found pragmatists who call themselves "liberal" and temper their convictions to suit the times. There are perhaps as many philosophers who saw things skewed by their own personal preferences but presented them to the world with unswerving force and dedication. These are the ideologues such as Marx, Nietzsche, Comte, and Mao Tse-tung.

Aquinas may not have stated anything about abortion in a direct manner. Nonetheless, a passage in his *Summa Theologica* speaks volumes about the human reality and inherent dignity of the unborn child: "Mary and Joseph needed to be instructed concerning Christ's birth before He was born, because it devolved on them to show reverence to the child conceived in the womb, and to serve Him even before He was born" (III, Q. 36, a. 2, ad.2). Since every Christian is called to imitate Christ, they are called to honor, with reverence, the Christ-child in the womb as well as all children in the womb. Here is another affirmation of the primacy of the child within the family. It was most fitting and appropriate for Mary and Joseph to revere the unborn Jesus. Therefore, the Holy Family, as the model family, is instructing all Christians (and everyone else, by extension) to revere the unborn child.

THE PEASANT PHILOSOPHER

Jacques Maritain

When his beloved wife and collaborator, Raissa, died in
1960, Jacques Maritain withdrew to a secluded life of
silence and prayer, living in a hut with the Little Brothers of
Jesus near the Garonne River at Toulouse, France. There, at
age eighty-five, he produced what he claimed to be his final
work: *The Peasant of the Garonne*.[18] The image pays tribute
to the peasant who dares to call a spade a spade. Philosophy
is a journey to wisdom, but one must honor the common
sense of the peasant to begin such a journey. In this respect,
he was true to his mentor St. Thomas Aquinas.

In his delightful book on St. Thomas Aquinas, G. K.
Chesterton declares that St. Thomas established his philosophy "on the universal common conviction that eggs are
eggs." Hegelians might have believed that eggs are really
what they will become: hens. Followers of Bishop Berkeley,

---

[18]   Jaques Maritian, *The Peasant of the Garonne: An Old Layman
     Questions Himself About the Present Time.* Translated by Michael
     Cuddihy and Elizabeth Hughes (New York, NY: Holt, Rinehart
     and Winston. 1968).

who rejected matter, would contend that eggs were merely dreams. Pragmatists would argue that the importance of eggs is their market price. "The Thomist," Chesterton maintains, "stands in the broad daylight of the brotherhood of men, in their common consciousness that eggs are not hens or dreams or mere practical assumptions; but things attested by the Authority of the Senses, which is from God." Maritain's identification with the peasant does not exclude him from philosophy but places him on its rightful path.

Jacques Maritain was born in Paris on November 18, 1882. He grew up in that city, barely nourished spiritually on the lukewarm Protestantism of his mother. When he entered the Lycée Henri IV, he possessed no particular religious convictions. He enrolled at the Sorbonne in 1901 during France's rich and corrupt Third Republic, a time when rabid French anti-clericalism had turned the Church into an intellectual ghetto. The school's rigid empiricism had effectively excluded any respectful discussion of spiritual matters. One day, as Jacques walked hand in hand through a Paris park with his Jewish girl friend, Raissa, the two made a pact that if, within a year, they could not find any meaning to life beyond the material, they would commit suicide.

That despair dissolved when they heard lectures at the Collège de France given by Henri Bergson, whose theories of creative evolution exalted the spirit of man and his ability to discover the intelligibility of things through intuition. In 1905, Jacques and Raissa, now newlyweds, met a passionate Catholic named Leon Bloy ("A Christian of the second century astray in the Third Republic") who led them into the Catholic faith.

Maritain soon began studying the massive works of St. Thomas Aquinas. As Aquinas had found in Aristotle a philosophical basis for harmonizing human reason with Christian faith, Maritain discovered in Aquinas possibilities for bringing a rejuvenated Thomism into a modern age of skepticism and science. "The disease afflicting the modern world," he wrote, "is above all a disease of the intellect." In one of his early works, *The Degrees of Knowledge*, Maritain sought to unify all the sciences and subdivisions of philosophy in the pursuit of reality.[19] Maritain was open to all trends and studied them carefully. He could do this, however, without ever losing sight of the perennial significance of philosophy. A close friend of his, the Russian existentialist Nikolai Berdyaev, accurately captured this feature of his esteemed colleague when he wrote these words about him in his autobiography: "He is very sensitive to new modern tendencies. But curiously enough, this has no effect on his philosophy."

At the height of his fame, in the 1920s and '30s, Maritain lectured at Oxford, Yale, Notre Dame, and Chicago. He also taught at Paris, Princeton, and Toronto. After World War II, he served three years as France's ambassador to the Vatican. In 1963 the French government honored him with its National Grand Prize for Letters.

The fifty or so books that Maritain wrote, spanning a period of more than half a century and translated into every major language, earned him the distinction of being "the greatest living Catholic philosopher."

---

19 Jacques Maritain, *Distinguish to Unite; or, The Degrees of Knowledge*. Translated from the 4th French ed. (New York: Scribner, 1959).

In his books, articles, and lectures, Maritain repeatedly and passionately called upon the Church to bring its theology and philosophy into contact with present day problems. His liberal thoughts concerning political and social justice issues won him bitter enemies among ultra-conventional Church thinkers. Attempts were even made, though unsuccessful, to have his books condemned by the Vatican.

Pope Paul VI honored Maritain during Vatican II, and in 1967 gave him unprecedented credit for inspiring the pontiff's landmark encyclical on economic justice, *Populorum Progressio*. He also considered making Maritain a cardinal, but the philosopher rejected the suggestion.

Maritain once referred to himself as "a man God has turned inside out like a glove." In a letter to poet Jean Cocteau, he wrote: "I have given my life to St. Thomas, and labor to spread his doctrine. For I, too, want intelligence to be taken from the Devil and returned to God." Indeed, no modern Catholic thinker has done more in an effort to achieve this end than Jacques Maritain. When he passed away in 1973, Pope Paul VI described him publicly as a "master of the art of thinking, of living, and of praying."

There has not appeared, since Maritain left the world, his equal as a lay Catholic philosopher.

To Love and Be Loved

Jean Vanier

Jean Vanier was born on September 10, 1928 in Geneva, Switzerland. His father, Major-General Georges Vanier, served as the nineteenth governor general of Canada. Jean received a broad education in Canada, England, and France. He served with the Royal Navy and the Royal Canadian Navy. He earned a doctorate in philosophy and taught at St. Michael's College at the University of Toronto. He produced his first book in 1966, *Happiness as Principle and End of Aristotelian Ethics.*

He was thirty-six years old and at a crossroad in his life. What goals would he pursue? He had aspired to be a naval officer. Yet, with his education, broad experience, and keen intelligence, he could have just as well sought a career as an academic, a foreign diplomat, or a writer. What motivated him, however, was more spiritual. It was as improbable as it was worthwhile.

In 1964, having left academia, he founded *L'Arche*, an international federation of communities for people with developmental disabilities and those who assist them. *L'Arche* is the French word for "(Noah's) Ark," a symbol of hope. Vanier had been appalled by the fact that people with developmental disabilities, especially those with Down syndrome, were institutionalized and therefore deprived of the dignity and respect that was their birthright. "We must do what we can to diminish walls, to meet each other," he stated. "Why do we put people with disabilities behind walls?"

The success of the *L'Arche* communities has been astonishing. Vanier has established no less than 147 of them in thirty-five countries. "I am struck," he explained, "by how sharing our weakness and difficulties is more nourishing to others than sharing our qualities and successes." Vanier understood that the desire to love and to be loved is something every person longs to experience. In 1971, he and Marie-Hélène Mathieu co-founded *Faith and Light* which also works for people with developmental disabilities. It has spread to over 1,800 communities in more than eighty countries.

For his work, Vanier has received numerous awards: the French Legion of Honour, the Templeton Prize, the Order of Canada, the *Pacem in Terris* Peace and Freedom Award, and the Community of Christ International Peace Award. Numerous high schools throughout Canada are named in his honor. On September 27, 2016, he received the Peace Abbey Foundation International Courage of Conscience Award for his lifelong commitment to building a world of inclusion for individuals with disabilities. His fame is not only international, but cosmic. In 2010 asteroid 8604 was officially named "Vanier" in his honor.

20

Vanier's immense success and the extravagant, though well-deserved praise that he has received, however, stands in stark contradiction with prevailing social attitudes toward people who have developmental disabilities. Attitudes toward the unborn who carry the gene for Down syndrome, for example, are light years from the acceptance and care that is characteristic of *L'Arche* and *Faith and Light*.

Down syndrome can be detected prenatally. According to the medical journal, *Prenatal Diagnosis* (Vol. 19, no. 1), 92 percent of Down syndrome confirmed pregnancies are aborted. In addition, when a Down syndrome baby is born, doctors often encourage the mother to abort the "defective" child and try again. One may recall how Sarah Palin was criticized for not aborting her Down syndrome daughter, Trig. Statistically, one out of every 691 babies in the United States is born with Down syndrome.

However, there is hope on the horizon. In March 2016, Indiana became the second state, after North Dakota, to ban abortions because of Down syndrome. Mike Pence, while governor of Indiana, signed the house bill which would ban doctors from knowingly aborting an unborn baby solely because of a genetic disability such as Down syndrome. Dr. Jérôme Lejeune, who discovered the genetic cause of Down syndrome, insisted that the medical establishment could find a cure for its unborn carriers if it did not spend its energy on killing them.

The realism and effectiveness of Vanier's working motto, "to love and be loved," is evidenced in many individual cases. One noteworthy example involves Dr. Harley Smyth, a world class neurosurgeon. When his daughter, Anna, was born with Down syndrome, some doctors suggested that he institutionalize her at three years of age when she was entitled to free medical care. The idea was repugnant to her father and prompted him to ask: "In the elimination of the obvious heartache involved in the receiving of a mentally retarded child into the family of man, what *else* might we eliminate?" That question was answered in a dramatic way, for the victim in waiting could very well have been Dr. Smyth himself.

He was fond of taking Anna, when she was seven years old, to an indoor pool for swimming lessons. One day at the pool she noticed a freckle on her father's back that looked different from the others. "Doctor fix it!" she said. Smyth asked a plastic surgeon at the hospital to examine the curious spot. The "freckle" turned out to be a malignant melanoma, an insidiously dangerous form of skin cancer, but caught by Anna at an early stage. In gratitude to his daughter for possibly saving his life (as well as the lives of Dr. Smyth's future patients), he would sometimes introduce himself at pro-life conferences as Anna's dad.

The contribution of Jean Vanier toward accepting people with developmental disabilities remains incomplete as long as they are routinely aborted precisely because of their condition. It is ardently hoped that the numerous schools named after Vanier honor him not only on their stationery, but in the classroom. Vanier has expressed his horror by the high rate of abortions for babies with Down syndrome.

Jean Vanier, who, even into his late eighties, has continued to live as a member of the original *L'Arche* community in Trosly-Breuil, France, fifty miles north of Paris. He has

authored some thirty books, dealing with philosophy, theology, tenderness, acceptance, tolerance, and love. With regard
to the latter, an abiding conviction of his is that "to love
someone is to show to them their beauty, their worth and
their importance." Amen.

Josef Pieper

Josef Pieper (1904–1997) was born in the Westphalian village of Elte, a town so isolated that no train was available to take any of its citizens to any other part of Westphalia. In order to reach the nearest train station, one had to cross a river in a small ferry-boat. Josef's father had the distinction of being the only teacher in the village's only school. Yet from Nazareth-like beginnings can come extraordinary accomplishments.

Josef attended school at the Gymnasium Paulinum in Münster, one of the oldest German schools, having served the cause of education for more than eleven hundred years. There, a priest teacher directed him to read the works of Saint Thomas Aquinas "with a sort of violent, ironical, and humorous intensity," as Pieper would later recall. He was eighteen at the time but had found his master and his life's guide. "St. Thomas is still my hero," wrote Pieper in the early 1950s. "I think his work is inexhaustible and his affirmative way of looking at the reality of the whole creation seems to me a necessary correction modern Christianity cannot do without."

In 1931, he wrote a few booklets on Pope Pius XI's encyclical *Quadragesimo Anno* and had planned to devote his career to the social sciences. However, it soon became impossible, with the emergence of National Socialism in Germany, for a Christian, let alone Catholic author, to speak in public on social issues. Pieper returned to his work in philosophy, applying the thought of Aquinas to the world in which he lived. And he did this with unusual clarity. "No one has written more wisely on the relation between thinking and doing than Pieper, yet there are no obstacles of erudition between the reader and the presentation," wrote philosopher Ralph McInerny. He earned T. S. Eliot's highest praise: "His sentences are admirably constructed, his ideas expressed with the maximum clarity. But his mind is submissive to what he believes to be the great, the main, tradition of European thought. . . . He restores to their position in philosophy what common sense obstinately tells us ought to be found there: insight and wisdom."

Pieper is most noted for his many books on virtue. In fact, he is commonly known as the "Philosopher of Virtue." Virtue for Pieper, following Aristotle and Aquinas, is perfective of the person. But the person is real and has an identifiable and intelligible nature. Wherever this nature is denied, totalitarianism gains a foothold. For, if there is no human nature, then there can be no crimes against it. Pieper, therefore, denounced the Nazi position that human rights and human dignity are based not on a common human nature but on ethnicity. Jean-Paul Sartre's famous declaration, "*Il n'y a pas de nature humaine,"* (there is no such thing as a human nature), perfectly exemplifies this unsupportable and unrealistic notion that human beings do not possess a common nature, that humanity is not universal. Thus, one can say with historian Jon Vickery that Pieper "may in fact be the man who said no to the spirit of his age."

According to Pieper, man's true humanness is what constitutes his goodness. And this humanness is "reason perfected in the cognition of truth." When truth is denied or neglected, the goodness of the human being is lost. "Whoever rejects truth, whether natural or supernatural, is really 'wicked' and beyond conversion," Pieper states in *The Four Cardinal Virtues*. Reason is understood as "regard for and openness to reality," and "acceptance of reality." Reason, reality, truth, nature, humanity, and goodness are all ordered to each other. The authentic or complete person cannot do without any of these factors. "Surrender to sensuality," he writes, "paralyzes the powers of the moral person."

In his time, virtue was either underappreciated, ignored, or neglected entirely, especially the virtue of courage. Pieper lived a long life and recognized clearly the impediments to virtue that assailed people living at the end of the twentieth century. "The restoration of man's inner eyes can hardly be expected in this day and age—unless, first of all, one were willing and determined simply to exclude from one's realm of life all those inane and contrived but titillating illusions incessantly generated by the entertainment industry."

If Pieper had lived well into the twenty-first century, how would he characterize the spirit of the present times and what remedies would he have proposed? He had observed that Modern Man "often calls lies and cowardice prudent, truthfulness and courageous sacrifice imprudent." Perhaps he would not be utterly surprised to find that abortion is now commonly regarded as merely a choice and that the aborting woman is simply being prudent. Nor would he be astonished to note that it is imprudent to point out that abortion is an instance of domestic violence that kills a member of the human family. With these observations in mind, he would insist on the importance of truth, whereas, during the rise of Nazism, he insisted on the importance of courage.

Pieper's contribution to truth is indeed timely. In a broader sense, however, truth is always timely because it is eternal. The truths that are particularly timely are precisely those that are rejected. What kind of person does Pieper have in mind who will work to re-introduce those truths that society lacks? Toward the end of his book *The Silence of Saint Thomas*, he remarks that "the truth will be more profoundly known *as* truth, the more vigorously its *timeliness* comes to light; it also means that a man experiencing his own time with a richer intensity of heart and fuller spiritual awareness has a better chance of experiencing the illuminating force of truth."

Josef Pieper offers us a model of a virtuous man who, while understanding the timelessness of truth, also understands how truth has a special timeliness at moments in history when certain truths are rejected or ignored. The true teacher, for Pieper, knows how, through "a constantly inquiring meditation, to discover and point out wherein lies the relevance of truth to his own time."

Father Adam Exner

"Saints are not people who plan and organize their particular style of life and perfection and follow it strictly on their own strength. Saints are people who love and trust God to the point that they let Him guide them and lead them where He wants." Adam Exner was not alluding to himself when he made this statement but to Saint Josemaria Escriva de Balaguer at the latter's canonization. Nonetheless, the comment could refer to him inasmuch as his life adventure, so implausible in purely sociological terms, demands a more supernatural explanation.

Adam Joseph Exner was born on Christmas Eve, 1928, at home on the family farm near Killaly, Saskatchewan. He was the last of eight children: five boys and three girls. His mother had a strong enough faith to give birth to him against her doctor's advice to abort. Although the pregnancy had its complications, the birth was uneventful. "How could I be anything but pro-life?" Exner would be able to tell audiences.

Exner's parents were Austrian immigrants. Making a living was a family enterprise. The Exners grew crops of grain and vegetables and raised livestock: chickens, turkeys, pigs, cattle, and horses. They were happy despite the absence of electricity, flush toilets, central heating, a radio, a TV, and a car. "My clothes were either hand-me-downs or homemade," he writes, in "A Faith Adventure." His overalls were made of denim cloth and shirts from bleached flour sack material. Despite such circumstances, he did not feel deprived. Besides, "life was the same for everyone."

It was *life* that the Exner family treasured. Human beings can endure many deprivations, but without life, they have nothing. With life, surrounded by love, they can be rich. Adam, like most young boys, had particular plans for his future. But an inner voice told him that they were not God's plans. That voice reminded him that one day he will meet his Creator who will ask, "What have you done with the gift of life I have given you?" Then and there, he knew what God was asking of him and he also knew that he would not be at peace until he was ready to dedicate his life to the service of God and his people. When he related this experience to his mother, she wept, for she had, indeed, been praying every day that God would lead one of her sons to the priesthood.

Nonetheless, it was not without considerable struggle that Adam was able to exchange his private dreams for God's plans. Later, looking back on his life, he could say, "The major orientations and directions in my life didn't come from me, but from God. In all truth, I can say with St. Paul, 'By the grace of God I am what I am.'" In the eyes of the world, his journey from a prairie farm to the Chancery in

Vancouver may be viewed as constituting a radical change. Certainly, his circumstances underwent an extreme change, but his commitment to the sanctity of life and the importance of the family remained as a stable element.

Adam Exner was ordained a priest of the Oblates of Mary Immaculate in1957. He was installed bishop of Kamloops, BC in 1974, archbishop of Winnipeg in 1982, and finally archbishop of Vancouver in 1991. He was professor, rector, and superior at St. Charles Scholasticate in Battleford, Saskatchewan and professor of moral theology at Newman Theological College in Edmonton, Alberta. Upon his retirement in 2004, the Catholic Civil Rights League created the Archbishop Exner Award for Catholic Excellence in his honor. I was most honored to be able to speak in behalf of Archbishop Exner's commitment to life when I received the award that bore his name in 2015.

Academically, Archbishop Exner holds degrees in philosophy and theology from the Pontifical Gregorian University in Rome and a doctoral degree in theology from the University of Ottawa. He speaks six languages: English, German, Italian, French, Spanish, and Latin. His learning was always at the service of life, the motto he adopted being "To Serve As He Served."

On May 11, 2017, at the age of eighty-eight, the archbishop emeritus, Adam Exner, spoke at a student's pro-life Mass in Victoria, BC. He based his talk on Jesus washing the feet of his closest followers. Jesus did this, Exner pointed out, to indicate that our mission as his followers is to serve others, the poor sick, the suffering, the vulnerable, and the marginalized. "And today," he asked, "who is in more need of our attention than the unborn child in the womb or the dying person who is suffering?" "Respect for human life," he went on to say, "especially to those in greatest difficulty, that is, to the unborn, and those near death, profoundly engages your mission both as young Catholics and as citizens of our democratic country. That's why we are participating in today's March for Life."

Refuting the weak rhetoric employed to support abortion, he explained that in opposing abortion, we are not "imposing" our religious beliefs on others, but "giving voice to values that are the common patrimony of all men and women, wherever they live and whoever they are." "You shall not kill" is not an arbitrary suggestion, but resonates within the deepest centers of our being. "It is on the hard-drive of humanity."

His final "tip" to his audience of "servants for life" was to remind them that the Holy Spirit is always working with them, that they are not alone. Therefore, "be courageous in swimming against the tide," a nautical event to which the archbishop had become thoroughly accustomed.

From a farm eight miles southeast of Killaly, Saskatchewan, to the Vancouver Chancery, for Exner, was not a geographical nor a sociological journey, but a spiritual one, guided by the Holy Spirit. He came a long way and through considerable hardship to tell us something he learned from a background of material deprivation; namely, that life and love are essential and all our service to others should be inspired by that fact.

The Making of a Philosopher

Stephen Schwarz

A new year arrives every twelve months; a new millennium, every twelve thousand months. In celebrating the latter, how does one begin to do justice to its magnitude? The rarity of the event demands something far more imaginative than noise makers and funny hats. There should be some serious reflection about life and the passing of time as one bids adieu to a thousand-year epoch and welcomes the inauguration of its successor.

Our hostess that evening of December 31, 1999 was up to the challenge. She distributed souvenir spoons to each of her guests and asked them to weave personal stories that each spoon evoked. Every spoon bore the name of a city. Mine was Munich, Germany, and was, indeed, a most propitious memory jogger.

On November 8, 1932, a philosopher colleague of mine, Stephen Schwarz, came into the world in that city. It was a time of grave political concern. Stephen's parents hosted meetings at their home to discuss, among friends, what might be done in such politically troublesome times. At the beginning of each meeting, Edith Stein, one of the guests, would come to the nursery and pick up little Stephen and hold him. No doubt she prayed for the child's health, his safety, and his future. To be held by a saint must be a most salutary experience. When, after reaching man's estate, Stephen informed me that he did not imbibe alcohol, I said, to his amusement, that for him "one Stein is enough."

Stephen and Edith would go their separate ways, Stephen to Harvard for his PhD in philosophy, Edith earning her doctorate at Freiburg, writing her dissertation on *The Problem of Empathy*. There can be no doubt that Edith had no problem with empathy in the nursery when she held baby Stephen. Later, Stephen took a philosophy position at the University of Rhode Island, Edith to Auschwitz and ultimately was canonized Saint Teresa Benedicta of the Cross.

Stephen's father, Balduin, found his way to philosophy through Dietrich von Hildebrand. As a student at the University of Munich, before he met von Hildebrand, he was dismayed to find that in the classes he was taking only historical philosophy prevailed; that is, philosophy in the manner of "Kant says . . . , Hegel says . . ." but never a word about what is really true. For it was truth that he was ardently seeking. Then he attended one of von Hildebrand's lectures. A new day dawned for him. Here was a man who dared to say what he saw as true. Here was truth, not just what so-and-so said. In the first five minutes of the first lecture he took from von Hildebrand, Balduin realized he had found what he was looking for. This is the true philosophy, he declared! This is what I want to pursue! This is my philosophical home! And this is the person I want to work under! A deep, life-long friendship ensued. Balduin formed his son in his philosophy, but he was able to do so only because von Hildebrand had first formed him. Von Hildebrand, therefore, was Stephen's philosophical grandfather.

Balduin bequeathed this approach to philosophy to his son and helped form his respect for the primacy of the dignity of life. According to Balduin, "The dignity of the person is the highest legal good (*Die Würde des Menschen ist das höchste Rechtsgut*)." This conviction represents the intellectual cornerstone in Stephen's book *The Moral Question of Abortion*[20] and his later book, co-authored with Kiki Latimer, *Understanding Abortion: From Mixed Feelings to Rational Thought.*[21]

Von Hildebrand's influence on the Schwarz family is considerable. He helped Stephen's mother abandon agnosticism and eventually become a Catholic. He also provided invaluable spiritual assistance to Stephen's grandfather. He was Stephen's godfather and held him as he was baptized. Stephen's middle name, appropriately, is Dietrich. He read from his philosophy to Stephen's mother as she was breast-feeding him. And so, writes, Stephen Schwarz, in a brief 2005 memoir, "his presence entered my being with my mother's milk."

I met Dr. Schwarz by chance at a pot-luck party in East Greenwich, Rhode Island. The first thing he said to me was, "I guess you got your promotion." As providence decreed, he

---

[20]   Stephen D.Schwarz, *The Moral Question of Abortion* (Chicago: Loyola University Press, 1990).

[21]   Stephen D.Schwarz and Kiki Latimer, *Understanding Abortion: From Mixed Feelings to Rational Thought* (Lanham, MD: Lexington Books, 2012).

had been randomly chosen to serve as a referee to evaluate my candidacy for promotion to full professor. It was the easiest decision of its kind he had ever made, he went on to say. What he particularly enjoyed was the fact that my chapter on "Generosity," in *The Heart of Virtue*,[22] was astonishingly similar to his father's treatment on that same virtue. I had not previously read anything by Balduin Schwarz.

Stephen Schwarz studied under von Hildebrand at Fordham University, taking as many courses from the master as he could. After class the two would continue their philosophical discussions on their way home, fifteen to twenty minutes on foot and thirty minutes on the subway. Stephen and his parents had fled Nazi Germany, arriving in New York City on June 27, 1941. A year earlier, Professor von Hildebrand arrived in the same city and secured an apartment for them, just below his at 448 Central Park West, right across from Central Park. In *The Moral Question of Abortion,* Dr. Stephen D. Schwarz acknowledges his debt to von Hildebrand: "It is mainly from him that I learned the art of philosophising as careful analysis of and faithfulness to reality."

Dr. Schwarz addresses a broad audience. He is at pains to present both sides of the abortion issue as evenly and objectively as possible. He gets to the heart of each position, the core idea from which it is developed, and leaves it to the reader to make up his or her own mind. Despite his meticulous attempt to be fair, as he once explained to me, some of his students would complain to him that he made the

---

22   Donald DeMarco, *The Heart of Virtue: Lessons from Life and Literature Illustrating the Beauty and Value of Moral Character* (San Francisco: Ignatius Press, 1996).

pro-life side more appealing. He found this kind of response more amusing than frustrating for it did not seem to occur to such students that the pro-life side is *inherently* more appealing because it is objectively more humane and realistic. And here is precisely where the philosopher comes in as the one who is not content merely to present an array of arguments, but to discover which argument reveals the truth of things. A philosopher must be more than an auditor. And a student must be more that a secretary.

I had the great privilege of teaching his daughter, Mary, who is also a philosopher. The souvenir spoon bearing the name "Munich" released a flood of memories that originated prior to the new millennium and predated additional memories that continue to weave a story that is, indeed, rich with providential implications.

PART III

Apostles From the World of Theology

Cardinal John O'Connor

I had finished giving a talk at Dunwoodie Seminary in Yonkers, New York when an aide came up to me and said, "The cardinal wants to see you." My first thought was, "What should I say to His Eminence?" To establish a common bound, I mentioned a friend of mine who had journeyed from Moose Jaw, Saskatchewan to New York with the hope of joining his newly created order, Sisters of Life. Not only did he remember her name, but details concerning her situation. We had an enjoyable chat and I was very much impressed by his keen memory and abiding concern for the people he has met.

Eight years earlier, John O'Connor returned from Rome with a red hat. Before he had a chance to deliver his first pro-life address as a cardinal (at the Hyatt Regency in Washington, DC), friends of his in the audience were clamoring for him to "put it on." "It doesn't fit," was his modest response. Cardinal O'Connor was indeed a modest man, but he was also courageous, a good combination of virtues to have if one is a Prince of the Church.

A friend of mine, in charge of organizing a pro-life conference, and without a great deal of appreciation for either protocol or practicality, called the chancery to invite the cardinal to be a guest-speaker. His secretary assured her that the invitation would be passed on to New York City's very busy archbishop. A few days passed. One evening when my friend was spending a leisurely evening at home, the phone rang: "This is Cardinal O'Connor. Thank you for inviting me to speak at your pro-life conference, but it seems that I have another engagement that day." She could hear, as she explained to me, the pages of his schedule book flutter as he turned to the date in question. He seemed apologetic about having to speak at the United Nations that day, but added, "I want you to know that what you are doing is very important and that I will pray for the success of your conference."

John Joseph O'Connor, the fourth of five children, was born on January 15, 1920 in a row house in a blue-collar Philadelphia neighborhood. He entered Charles Borromeo Seminary when he was sixteen and was ordained nine years later. After working as a parish priest for seven years, he entered the Navy and served as a chaplain for twenty-seven years, rising to Rear Admiral and Chief of Chaplains. He was appointed bishop of Scranton, PA in 1983 and held that post for less than a year when he was chosen to succeed Cardinal Cook as archbishop of New York.

Throughout his varied career, one thing defined his ministry: the sanctity of life. Yet his concern for life went beyond abortion. He inaugurated annual celebrations for people with disabilities and promoted workers' causes. In 1988 he donated all his Social Security earnings as long as he lived, to a scholarship fund he started for African American students. He visited AIDS patients at an archdiocesan hospital and could be found listening to them, cleaning their sores, and changing their bedpans.

His legacy, nonetheless, will center on his thought and actions with respect to abortion. Gentleness always characterized his approach to this hotly contested issue. In a pamphlet entitled *Abortion: Questions & Answers,* he writes, "When our message is heard—the message of life and love for both mother and child—I believe most Americans, whatever their religious persuasion, will want to join in a commitment to the sacredness of every human life." Contrary to the view of many Americans, who think that the right to life is conferred by the state, the cardinal reasons that life has its own intrinsic value; life is sacred in itself. Accordingly, "the state has as its primary purpose the defense of the lives of its citizens." The cardinal then quotes America's third president who remarked that life is "the first and only legitimate object of good government—the care of human life, and not its destruction."

At the conclusion of a lengthy address he delivered at Cathedral High school on October 15, 1984, he made the plea "that all women and men of good will try to open their minds and hearts to at least the possibility that we are unjustifiably taking 4,000 innocent human lives each day, regardless of whatever convictions they may hold to the contrary." It was a most gentle urging to begin at least thinking about a stupendous problem.

Realizing that no one person can turn the abortion tide, Cardinal O'Connor founded Sisters of Life in June of 1991. He understood that over the course of history religious communities were formed to meet the special needs of the day. And that special interest, in his mind, is in working to restore a sense of the sacredness of life. There are, at this writing, more than one hundred members of the order who offer days of prayer and healing to women (and men) who have been harmed by abortion. They also provide retreats for those working in the pro-life movement.

John Cardinal O'Connor entered the next life on May 3, 2000. In his final days, he spoke of experiencing "unutterable peace." During his homily at the cardinal's funeral, Boston's Cardinal Law inspired a standing ovation when he said of his beloved friend: "What a legacy he has left us in his consistent reminder that the Church must always be unambiguously pro-life. . . . Perhaps his most lasting testament in support of life will be the work of the Sisters of Life, a religious community he founded and loved so dearly."

Regard for the sanctity of life is fundamental in both the life of the individual and in the spirit of a nation. It represents a conviction one can firmly hold without fear of it being dismissed as arbitrary, judgmental, radical, conservative, or even religious. It is a conviction that coincides with a person's sense of who he is as a human being.

Saint Teresa Benedicta of the Cross

Most Catholics are familiar, more or less, with the outline of Edith Stein's life. She was the youngest of eleven children born on October 12, 1891 in Breslau, Germany to devout Jewish parents. Her mother knew about life's hardships, having lost four children during the early years of her marriage. Frau Auguste Stein was the formative influence in Edith's development. Nonetheless, between the ages of thirteen and twenty-one, as Edith confessed, she could not believe in a personal God. Through many twists and turns, however, Edith became a Catholic and eventually a Carmelite nun, taking the name Teresa Benedicta of the Cross. Because of her Jewish heritage, she was arrested by the Nazis and taken to Auschwitz where she, along with her sister Rosa, met their deaths. She was canonized on Sunday, October 11, 1998. In his homily on that occasion, Pope John Paul II remarked, "Today . . . we bow to the memory of Edith Stein, proclaiming the indomitable witness she bore during her life and especially by her death. Now alongside

Teresa of Avila and Thérèse of Lisieux, another Teresa takes her place among the host of saints who do honor to the Carmelite Order."

Toward the end of her life, she considered herself as one of the countless "hidden souls" who remain hidden from the whole world. She was a philosopher of distinction and a superb translator. She wrote poetry and was an excellent teacher. She earned honors as a nurse and was a loving companion for her many family members including all of her many nieces and nephews. Much of her intellectual work is esoteric and remains hidden from both the world as well as from most Catholics. She will be better remembered for her courage and her faith, and how she could find peace in the midst of desolation. Perhaps her model as a true feminist will be one of her most important legacies, especially for women who are troubled about their identity and their vocation.

At the beginning of her extensive essay "On the Nature of Woman," she makes a point that is as simple and straightforward as it is profound and worthy of meditation: "The vocation of man and woman is not quite the same in the original order, the order of fallen nature and the order of redemption." In the original order, the relationship between man and woman was intended to be one of pure, loving communion. As a result of Original Sin, their relationship lost this purity and became tainted by lust and a mistaken sense of inequality. Redemption by Christ is needed so that man and woman can return to the original order.

This opening sentence reveals three important characteristics of Saint Teresa Benedicta: her faith in the authenticity of

Scripture, her unblinking realism in the face of extreme evil, and her hope that ultimately good will prevail. The adoption of these three virtues is her prayer for today's women of the world.

If Scripture is ignored or rejected, women will not have a basis on which they can understand their true nature. As a result, they will begin their understanding of themselves from something that has been broken. At that point, it is inevitable that they will find wholly external reasons for their fallen state. They will blame politics, economics, their upbringing, or men. But not realizing that they have fallen from what they should be, they tend to neglect the arduous task of self-improvement.

Both men and women have been wounded by the Fall, but their identities have not been entirely lost. "Owing to the close relationship between mother and child," Saint Teresa Benedicta writes, "and woman's special capacity for sharing and devoting herself to another's life, she will have the principal part in education." Edith Stein wrote her doctoral thesis on the topic of "empathy," utilizing her feminine gifts to complete a scholarly assignment which at her time, was considered to be the exclusive province of the male. At the same time, always concerned about balance, she states that "the demands of motherhood make it imperative that man should protect and care for mother and child."

A virtuous life demands that we remain close neighbors. Sympathy for the problems of others is natural for the woman. But this fine inclination can be perverted, as she remarks, when a woman behaves as "the interfering busybody that cannot tolerate silent growth and thus does not foster development, but hinders it." Sympathy can be distorted in many other ways, for example, "by an unmeasured interest on others which shows itself as curiosity, gossip, and an indiscreet longing to penetrate into the lives of other people."

The battle of the sexes will continue unabated unless men and women look to a supernatural remedy. "This transcending of natural barriers," she writes, "is the highest effect of grace; it can never be achieved by carrying on a self-willed struggle against nature and denying its barriers, but only by humble subjection to the divine order."

Edith Stein spent a great deal of her active life among male scholars. She advises women that their womanhood is far stronger than their environment or the people who populate it. Whether she is a mother, a nun, or a professional working in the world, a woman preserves, protects, and develops her feminine genius by modelling herself "as the Mother of God had been in all the circumstances of her life, whether she was living as a virgin in the sacred precincts of the Temple, silently keeping house at Bethlehem and Nazareth, or guiding the apostles and the first Christian community after the death of her Son."

The three Carmelite saints mentioned in Pope John Paul II's canonization homily offer a rich and realistic meditation on what it means to be a woman in the best sense. They provide something far deeper and more authentic than what the world can offer. The influence of Saint Teresa Benedicta of the Cross will not remain hidden, because it is conjoined with the divine life that fills the soul.

Pope Benedict XVI

Joseph Aloysius Ratzinger was born to a devout Catholic family on April 16, 1927 in the village of Marktl am Inn in Bavaria. He came into the world on Holy Saturday on the feast day of Benedict Joseph Labré, who was canonized in 1883 by Pope Leo XIII. When he was five years old, Joseph declared that he wanted to become a priest.

In 1933 Hitler came into power and ushered in a reign of horror. A cousin of Joseph's had Down syndrome. In 1941, when the boy was roughly the same age as Joseph, Nazi officials came and took him away for "therapy." He never came back. He was murdered as part of the Action T4 campaign of Nazi eugenics. He was considered one of the many who were deemed "undesirable" "defective," or "useless eaters" and therefore had to be permanently removed from society.

The notion that certain human beings could be classified as something less than human remained with Joseph Ratzinger throughout his life. He recognized that what undergirds various attempts to dehumanize people—from the Nazi ideology to more current ideologies that rationalize abortion, embryo research, physician-assisted suicide, and euthanasia—is a disregard for the dignity of the human person. The truth of the human being became a dominant and permanent concern in Ratzinger's mind.

When Ratzinger became bishop in 1977, he chose the motto "Cooperators of the truth." As he stated, "I chose that motto because in today's world the theme of truth is omitted almost entirely, as something too great for man, and yet everything collapses if truth is missing." Accordingly, as Ratzinger went on to explain, it is not enough to defeat Hitler. One must reinstate truth. In the contemporary world, when the sanctity of human life—which is at the core of the truth of man—is omitted and replaced an abstract notion of "choice," a swarm of assaults against life ensue. Ratzinger was acutely aware of the philosophical roots of the problem.

He carried this concern for the truth of the human being through his years as prefect of the Sacred Congregation of the Faith (1981–2005) and into his papacy. He saw clearly the inadequacy of relativism as a replacement for truth, explaining how it led inevitably to what he called the "dictatorship of relativism." He was also keenly aware of how academia is not an ally of truth, often claiming that it is either unattainable or non-existent. Relativism, skepticism, nihilism, and deconstructionism were commonplace in universities.

As prefect of the Sacred Congregation of the Faith, he made perhaps his most important defense of human life, in that capacity, with the release of *Donum Vitae* ("Instruction on Respect for Human Life in its Origins and on the Dignity of Procreation," 1987). The instruction reaffirms the inseparable connection between the unitive and procreative dimensions of the marital act. Artificial technologies that replace the conjugal act lead to regarding the child conceived as an object rather than as a gift of God. Technologies that assists but does not replace the marital act are licit. Thus, surgically opening a blocked fallopian tube can be licit, while *in vitro* fertilization is not. Essentially, the instruction holds to the position that both life (in its origin or at its conception) and the conjugal act have great dignity and that neither of these two dignities can be compromised in any way. The instruction describes truth about new life and the truth of the conjugal act.

Because truth is the factor that illuminates who human beings are and how they should live, it is far more reliable than emotion, convenience, or desperation. Accordingly, the then Cardinal Ratzinger stated that *Donum Vitae* is relevant to everyone: "In the light of the truth about the gift of human life, and in the light of the moral principles which follow from the truth, everyone is invited to act in the area of responsibility proper to each and, like the good Samaritan, to recognize as a neighbor even the littlest among the children of men."

As Pope Benedict XVI, he returned once again to the theme of truth in his 2009 encyclical *Caritas in Veritate*: "The natural law, in which creative Reason shines forth, reveals our greatness, but also our wretchedness insofar as we fail to recognize the call to moral truth." Trying to live without the light of Reason, is like trying to read a book in the dark. It is a strange characteristic of modern man that he often prefers something other than the light of reason and the guidance of truth to navigate through the various challenges and obstacles that life presents.

Reason, of course, which needs to be "purified," is a word he uses several times in his 2005 encyclical *Deus Caritas Est*. In one instance, he states that "if reason is to be exercised properly, it must undergo constant purification, since it can never be completely free of the dangers of a certain ethical blindness caused by the dazzling effect of power and special interest." Although reason and truth are not as readily accessible as apples are on an apple tree, they are nonetheless indispensable. Additional work is required so that reason is purified and truth is deepened. To use reason to provide rationalizations is to use reason to the exclusion of truth.

Cardinal Ratzinger and Karol Wojtyla did not meet each other until 1978 at the first conclave. Philosophically and theologically they had much in common and agreed on the challenges of the time and the need to recapture the joy and authenticity of the Second Vatican Council. As George Weigel documents in his monumental biography of St. John Paul II, *Witness to Hope*, they both understood the necessity to inform the world that the Gospels represent Truth. Weigel goes on to say that Wojtyla recognized in the shy, scholarly Ratzinger a contemporary intellectual who was a more accomplished theologian than himself. Together they made a formidable intellectual team. Toward the end of his life. Pope St. John Paul II referred to Cardinal Ratzinger as "my trusted friend."

Saint Teresa of Kolkata

"I feel the greatest destroyer of peace today is abortion, because it is a direct war, a direct killing, direct murder by the mother herself. And we read in the scripture, for God says very clearly: 'Even if a mother could forget her child, I will not forget you. I have carved you in the palm of my hand.' We are carved in the palm of his hand; so close to him, that unborn child has been carved in the hand of God."

These words were spoken by Mother Teresa as part of her acceptance speech when she received the coveted Nobel Peace Prize (December 11, 1979). The words of a saint should not be taken lightly. Nor should her actions. Mother Teresa donated the $192,000 prize money to build homes for the destitute, especially for the lepers. Her generosity was perfectly consistent with the standards the five-member Nobel Committee of the Norwegian Parliament in Oslo used in determining their 1979 Nobel Laureate for Peace: "This year, the world has turned its attention to the plight of children and refugees, and these are precisely the categories for whom Mother Teresa has for many years worked so successfully."

Nearly four decades after the now-sainted Mother Teresa gave her acceptance speech, abortion—the destroyer of peace—is more pervasive than ever before. Moreover, its rationalizations, in many instances, have assumed a totalitarian status. A situation at a Catholic university provides a chilling example of this phenomenon. Stéphane Mercier is a philosophy teacher at the Catholic University of Louvain in Belgium. In the spirit of a good philosopher, he has asked his students to reflect on the abortion issue and to challenge media rhetoric. In a paper he distributed, he wrote the following, not as if it represented the "right" position, but as a means of stimulating thought: "The murder of an innocent person capable of defending himself is revolting; but to attack someone who does not have the strength or the resources to defend himself is even more dreadful." One might fairly recognize these words as constituting a truism. Nonetheless, it aroused the ire of a group of feminists who notified university officials. As a result, the school saw fit to suspend Stéphane Mercier from his teaching duties. The case was placed under investigation. In its defense, school officials proclaimed that "in the spirit of the 1990 Act decriminalizing abortion," the school "respects the autonomy of women to make this choice, in the circumstances specified by the legislator." Philosophy, to say the least, must be more than a blind acceptance of the law.

The world, if it is at all interested in peace, needs the words and wisdom of Saint Teresa of Kolkata. In 1994 Mother Teresa drew from her Nobel Prize acceptance speech at the

National Prayer Breakfast before President Clinton and his wife, Hillary. "But I feel that the greatest destroyer of peace today is abortion," she said, "because it is a war against the child, a direct killing of the innocent child, murder by the mother herself. And if we accept that a mother can kill even her own child, how can we tell other people not to kill one another? How do we persuade a woman not to have an abortion?" Mother Teresa could not have been more politically incorrect nor more courageous.

Wall Street Journal writer Peggy Noonan was present at the breakfast and had this to say concerning the reactions to Mother Teresa's words on the part of the president and the first lady and the vice-president and his wife: "But not everyone applauded. The president and first lady, seated within a few feet of Mother Teresa on the dais, were not applauding. Nor were the vice president and Mrs. Gore. They looked like seated statues at Madame Tussaud's. They glistened in the lights and moved not a muscle, looking at the speaker in a determinedly semi-pleasant way."

Lady Gaga would not have been treated so coldly. The path to peace in our beleaguered world may not be illuminated by its present leaders, either those who have political power and those who preside over universities. Mother Teresa is a true humanitarian. She loves people and lives by the Golden Rule. In her own way, as a servant of God, she has become, in spite of herself, a leader. In 1950 she founded the Missionaries of Charity, a religious order of sisters who care for the poorest of the poor throughout the world. Today there are approximately 4,500 of these sisters worldwide who are continuing the work of Mother Teresa, serving in hospices, orphanages, homes for people with AIDS, those who suffer from drug addictions, and others who need loving care. There is no rift between Mother Teresa's words and her actions.

The path to peace begins with silence and proceeds through golden landmarks along the way. It is mapped out on what Mother Teresa has called her "business card": "The fruit of silence is prayer. The fruit of prayer is faith. The fruit of faith is love. The fruit of love is service. The fruit of service is peace." St. Augustine referred to peace as "the tranquility of order." Mother Teresa has spelled out this order for us in a specific way. If the world wants peace, it must also want its preambles in the form of silence, prayer, faith, love, and service. The path is simple, but how many people are willing to set foot on such a path?

Mother Teresa died in Kolkata in 1997 at the age of eighty-seven. On September 4, 2016, the woman who was born in Albania as Agnes Gonxha Bojaxhiu was canonized Saint Mother Teresa before a gathering of 120,000 people in St. Peter's Square. Pope Francis, presiding at the event, told the audience and the world that "Mother Teresa, in all aspects of her life, was a generous dispenser of divine mercy, making herself available for everyone through her welcome and defense of human life, those unborn and those abandoned and discarded."

Saint John Paul II

Jarosław Kupczak, OP, has produced an excellent study on the thought of John Paul II entitled *Destined for Liberty.*[23] On the very last page, the author asks whether history will honor John Paul as "The Great." This encomium, to be sure, is awarded most sparingly. Only Popes Leo I and Gregory I have been so honored.

Fr. Kupczak quotes George Weigel, who has informed us that both of history's "Great" pontiffs had one thing in common that was a claim to their distinguished title. Each was successful in resisting the threats of barbarians. Leo turned Attila the Hun back from Rome; Gregory effected a truce with the invading Lombards and then set to work converting them to orthodox Christianity.

Weigel proposes that John Paul's claim to greatness has much in common with his towering predecessors.

---

23   Jarosław Kupczak, *Destined for Liberty: The Human Person in the Philosophy of Karol Wojtyła/John Paul II* (Washington, DC: Catholic University of America Press, 2000).

97

"This time," Weigel argues, "the barbarians are the modern and post-modern 'masters of suspicion,' whose radical deconstruction of reason poses a grave threat to Western civilization."

John Paul makes reference to the "Masters of Suspicion" (*maître du soupçon*), borrowing the expression from philosopher Paul Ricoeur, in his "Theology of the Body." These "suspicious" characters are Nietzsche, Marx, and Freud, who are staunch and influential advocates of the Deadly Sins of Pride, Envy, and Lust, respectively.

The new barbarians, therefore, are intellectuals who have invaded the precincts of the human mind with deadly ideas. The modern world has trouble identifying them because it has stereotyped barbarians as being uneducated, unsophisticated, and illiterate roughnecks. Those who are included in the broad ambit of "The Masters of Suspicion," including the vast horde of Nietzscheans, Marxists, and Freudians, and more, are, as a matter of fact, well educated, sophisticated, and highly literate.

The old barbarians attacked the body; the new barbarians attack the mind. We must broaden our understanding of what it means to be a barbarian, for today's barbarian has undergone a complete fashion change, or, in popular parlance, "a total makeover." The new barbarian is clothed in sheepskin and is a cunning strategist.

The word *barbarian* originated when ancient Greeks heard people speaking in languages other than their own. Naturally, they found these alien tongues to be utterly incomprehensible. But they ridiculed what they could not comprehend, derisively referring to foreigners as simply mouthing "bar-bar." The irony here, of course, is that it was those who did the ridiculing who were the barbarians, not necessarily the foreigners.

Barbarism, therefore, is attacking or dismissing what we do not understand simply because we do not understand it. When Stanford University students chanted, "Hey, hey, ho, ho, Western civ has got to go," it should be clear who the barbarians were.

Dr. Carl Henry, in *Twilight of a Great Civilization*,[24] writes: "A half-generation ago the pagans were still largely threatening at the gates of Western culture; now the barbarians are plunging into the . . . mainstream. As they seek to reverse the inherited intellectual and moral heritage of the Bible . . . we are engaged as never before in a rival conflict for the mind, the conscience, the will, the spirit, the very selfhood of contemporary man."

It is as if the new barbarians are suffering from an advanced form of semantic aphasia, no longer able to comprehend the meaning of marriage, motherhood, fatherhood, morality, conscience, person, rights, duties, virtue, good, evil, truth, beauty, and the very meaning of life. But in rejecting their intellectual and moral inheritance, they cover themselves with the mantel of barbarism.

It appears that the new barbarians, lost in a fog of relativism, paralyzed by political correctness, and submissive to the demands of self-centered students, myopic administrations, and meretricious publishing houses, have quietly slipped

---

[24]   Carl F. H. Henry, *Twilight of a Great Civilization: The Drift Toward Neo-Paganism* (Westchester, Ill: Crossway Books, 1988).

into barbarism without even noticing the transmogrification they have undergone. The beautiful butterfly has reverted to a crawling caterpillar.

Against the new barbarians, John Paul has provided a solid, consistent, comprehensive, down-to-earth description of the human being. He has enlisted the insights of literature, art, philosophy, history, psychology, and theology to shed light on the nature of the human being. As his retort to the new barbarians, Fr. Kupzcak concludes, "John Paul II created his Christian anthropology." This is his "personalism," his "anthropological realism," his concerted effort to provide an understanding of who we are as human beings so that we will have a firm basis on which to direct our moral lives. Unless we know who we are, we will not know what we are supposed to do.

Nowhere is contemporary barbarism more evident than in the life issues, especially with regard to abortion. Advocates of abortion have changed language to suit their ideology. The unborn child is merely a "fetus," abortion is a "termination" or "a second chance to practice contraception," the abortionist is a "health care provider," and so forth. John Paul's language is direct and unvarnished. Accordingly, the Holy Father states, in *Evangelium Vitae*, that democracies that deny the inalienable right to life of any human being from conception to natural death are "tyrant states." "Abortion and euthanasia are," he boldly asserted, "crimes which no human law can claim to legitimize."

He reminds his readers that the commandment concerning the inviolability of human life is clearly stated in the covenant of Sinai: "You shall not kill" (Ex 20:13); "Do not slay the innocent and righteous" (Ex 23:7). The New Testament is a refinement of these negative commands and emphasizes the positive: "You shall love your neighbor as yourself" (Rm 13:9–10). Consequently, "the deepest element of God's commandment to protect human life is *the requirement to show reverence and love* for every person and the life of every person."

Evangelium Vitae, therefore, is essentially a positive document, urging the building up of a Culture of Life based on love. It is also one that reaches out to a wide spectrum of humanity, to "all people of good will." Kenneth Woodward, religion editor of *Newsweek,* hailed it as "the clearest, most impassioned and most commanding encyclical of John Paul's pontificate. He believed that it would be the Holy Father's "signature statement" in history. The claim can be justly made that the now sainted pontiff is, if not John Paul "the Great," then surely the greatest Apostle of Life that has appeared on the modern stage.

The Immortal Chaplains

The word *courage* is derived from Old French (*corage*), Modern French (*coeur*), as well as Latin (*cor*). All of these words refer to the heart. Now since the heart symbolizes love, true courage must be an expression of love. Just as there is a paradoxical relationship between life and death, so too, the same obtains between love and courage. How does one begin to understand this apparent contradiction? The soldier, surrounded by danger, needs to combine a strong desire for living with a certain readiness to die. If he clings too tenaciously to life, he is a coward. If he rushes headlong into death, he is a fool. But if he has genuine courage, as the master of the paradox G. K. Chesterton asserts, "he must desire life like water and yet drink death like wine." We do not honor the suicide who prefers death to life, but we do honor the hero who accepts death while displaying his love for life. Christ testifies to the validity of this paradox when he tells us that there is no greater love than to lay down your life for a friend (Jn 15:13). Four chaplains, each uniformed in military dress and all of the same heart, have beautifully and heroically illustrated the legitimacy of this paradox.

On January 23, 1943, the S. S. Dorchester, carrying 904 passengers, mostly military men, left for Greenland. During the early morning hours of February 3, 1943, the ship was torpedoed by the German submarine *U-223* off the coast of Newfoundland. The blast knocked out the electrical system, leaving the ship in the dark. Panic ensued. Four chaplains sought to calm the men and organize an orderly evacuation. They also assisted in the attempt to guide the wounded men to safety. Life jackets were passed out until the limited supply ran out. The chaplains then removed their own life jackets and gave them to others. They helped as many men as they could into lifeboats. When they could no longer be of help, they linked arms, saying prayers and singing hymns. They went down with the ship. Two ships that accompanied the Dorchester, disobeying orders to continue the search for the German U-Boat, stopped and rescued 230 men from the frigid waters. Nearly 700 perished, making it the third largest loss at sea of its kind for the United States during World War II.

The four chaplains were of different faiths but shared the conviction that there is no greater love than to lay down your life for a friend. One survivor provided a moving testimony: "The last thing I saw, the Four Chaplains were up there praying for the safety of the men. They had done everything they could. I did not see them again. They themselves did not have a chance without their life jackets." According to the testimony of another survivor: "I could hear men crying, pleading, praying. I could also hear the chaplains preaching

courage. Their voices were the only thing that kept me going."
According to the Army War College account, another survivor of the Dorchester, John Ladd, said of the four chaplains'
selfless act: "It was the finest thing I have seen or hope to see
this side of heaven." According to some reports, survivors
could hear different languages mixed in the prayers of the
chaplains, including Jewish prayers in Hebrew and Catholic
prayers in Latin.

Who were these courageous and self-sacrificing men?
They were truly an extraordinary quartet. George L. Fox
was a Methodist preacher who had been decorated for bravery and was awarded the Silver Star, Purple Heart, and the
French Croix de Guerre. Alexander D. Goode, the son of
a Rabbi, followed in his father's footsteps. He received his
PhD from Johns Hopkins University. He was both an athlete as well as an intellectual. Clark V. Poling was ordained in
the Reformed Church of America. He studied at Yale University's Divinity School and graduated with a BD degree
in 1936. John P. Washington was a Catholic priest. He was
Chief of the Chaplains Reserve Pool in Fort Benjamin Harrison, Indiana. In 1942, he reported to Camp Myles Standish
in Taunton, Massachusetts where he met Chaplains Fox,
Goode, and Poling at Chaplains School at Harvard.

On December 19, 1944, all four chaplains were awarded
the Purple Heart and the Distinguished Service Cross,
posthumously. In 1988, February 3 was established by a
unanimous act of Congress as an annual "Four Chaplains
Day." The United States Post Office Department issued a
commemorative stamp in 1948 honoring the chaplains.
The issue was unusual in that US stamps were not normally

minted to honor someone other than the president of the United States until at least ten years after his or her death. Their names were replaced by the words: "These immortal chaplains . . . Interfaith in Action." The Four Chaplains Memorial Foundation is located at the former South Philadelphia Navy Yard. Its official mission statement is "to further the cause of 'unity without uniformity' by encouraging goodwill and cooperation among all people." The various ways in which these self-sacrificing men of God are honored, in music, literature, iconography, and other modes of expression, is quite extensive. For a more complete account of the four chaplains, one can read *No Greater Glory: The Four Immortal Chaplains and the Sinking of the Dorchester in World War II* by Dan Kurzman.[25]

We often admire what we are reluctant to imitate. Nonetheless, our willingness to honor genuine heroes at least keeps our sights on the right ideal. Perhaps this is the first step in gaining the willingness to do something heroic. In the meantime, there are the unheroic acts of self-sacrifice that are always within our grasp. One way of honoring the "Immortal Chaplains" and their like is by making the small acts of generosity. That may very well have been the apprenticeship of chaplains Fox, Goode, Poling, and Washington long before they boarded the ill-fated S. S. Dorchester.

---

[25]   Dan Kurzman, *No Greater Glory: The Four Immortal Chaplains of World War II and the Sinking of the Dorchester* (New York: Random House, 2004).

William May

After the release of *Humanae Vitae* in 1968, dissent became rampant in the Catholic Church, especially in America. Undergirding dissent was the presumption that dissenters were expressing their freedom and their courage in speaking out against traditional Church teaching. These two presumptions, however, must be called into question since the dissenters, if they were sincere, would have extended these two qualities to anyone who expressed his freedom and courage to assent to Church teaching. Such, to a large extent, was not the case. Dissent was not only allowed but applauded if it were against the Church. But dissenting from the dissenters, in many cases, was a punishable offense. In fact, dissent became the litmus test for job security in certain Catholic universities.

Every injustice sparks heroes. Perhaps the most war-tested among those who had the temerity to speak against the dissenters was Dr. William E. May, who ended his formal teaching career at the Pontifical Institute for Studies on

Marriage and Family in Washington, DC. His odyssey from outcast to recipient of the *Pro Ecclesia et Pontifice* medal, the highest honor a lay person can receive from the pope, demonstrates the fact that true freedom and courage is on the side of assent to Church teaching.

The trajectory of the principal dissenter, Fr. Charles E. Curran, on the other hand did not fare so well. After a seventeen-year investigation, the Vatican Congregation of the Doctrine of the Faith concluded that Father Charles Curran should no longer be eligible to exercise the function of a professor of Catholic theology. As a result, Curran was suspended from his duties as a professor of moral theology at the Catholic University of America.

I had the pleasure and honor of knowing Professor May. He had a rare condition called heterochromia, characterized by the irises of his eyes being of different colors, an anomaly shared by celebrities such as Jane Seymour and Dan Aykroyd. But there was nothing anomalous about his vision. He saw clearly the reasonable grounds on which Pope Paul VI established his controversial encyclical *Humanae Vitae* and expressed it clearly, often convincingly, to his students, readers, and various associates. I once asked him what it was like teaching alongside of Charles Curran and other dissenters in the theology department at Catholic University. "Trench warfare," was his immediate and candid response. No doubt it was in that battlefield that his understanding of why the Church objected to contraception, abortion, euthanasia, technologically assisted forms of reproduction, and homosexual acts was refined and sharpened so that he could better share his wisdom with others through his teaching and through his writing.

One of May's former students, who became a professor of moral theology at a Catholic seminary, was not indulging in hyperbole when he said of his mentor, "He inspired a generation of younger moralists, including myself, to follow his courageous example in defending and explicating Catholic moral teaching in its entirety, including in its more unpopular dimensions." John Finnis, a scholar and close friend, credited May with a basket full of virtues, including "frankness, energy, quickness of mind, hard work, zeal for the Lord, and courtesy to all."

Nonetheless, his teaching was not appreciated by everyone. When he refused to stop teaching in support of *Humanae Vitae*, the department at Catholic University fired him five years after he had been hired. However, he was awarded tenure by a single vote in the Catholic University of America's Graduate School of Theology.

May was a sound thinker and an excellent scholar. He cited an argument against contraception from the writings of Saint John Chrysostom: "Why do you sow where the field is eager to destroy the fruit? . . . Do you contemn the gift of God, and fight with his law?" From the writings of John Calvin, he culled the following: "The voluntary spilling of semen outside of intercourse between a man and a woman is a monstrous thing." After marshalling an extensive list of pertinent citations from various authors, May came to the conclusion that "contraception, we have now seen, is the 'gateway' to the culture of death."

In an article entitled "Charles E. Curran's Grossly

Inaccurate Attack on the Moral Theology of John Paul II," May delineates several "utterly false" premises upon which Curran mounts his arguments. He concludes, with the support of a list of sociologists, that Pope Paul VI was truly prophetic: the use of contraception does, in fact, lead to greater infidelity within marriage and more sex outside of marriage, despite what Catholic dissenters predicted to the contrary. In a book which May edited, *Vatican Authority and American Catholic Dissent,* he reminds his readers that public questioning by a theologian of Church teaching on a particular issue does not "usurp the teaching authority of the magisterium." Dissent, therefore, is merely dissent, and does not replace Church teaching. Some of the dissenters, nonetheless, wanted their dissent to provide a "second magisterium." Moreover, while May was applying scholarship to the issues at hand, Curran was utilizing the media to propagate the presumed glamour associated with being a dissenter.

May became well known and highly respected. He participated in scholarly meetings and/or gave public lectures in Rome, Vatican City, Barcelona, Pamplona, Toronto, Oxford, Manila, Singapore, Puerto Rico, Mexico, Ireland, Austria, India, New Zealand, and Australia, as well as in many venues in the United States. He was a member of seven scholarly organizations and was president of the Fellowship of Catholic Scholars from 1985–87.

In our final telephone conversation, he told me how pleased he was to be able to teach a group of residents at the retirement home in which they resided, though from a wheel chair and despite being handicapped with various infirmities. He mentioned, with justifiable pride, that all of his seven children became medical doctors. One of his former students, who visited May on a nearly daily basis, recalled Bill's trust in God amid great physical suffering over the final seven years. "I can still hear his voice saying, 'God is so good to me.'"

William E. May passed away on December 13, 2014, at eighty-six years of age. It was the fifty-seventh anniversary to the day when he and his future wife, Patricia, first met.

Father Richard Neuhaus

Fr. Neuhaus (1936–2009) combined the moral virtues of forthrightness and fearlessness with the literary skills of fine phrasing and wry humor. Two examples serve the point: "[One] frequently encounters in the same person an awesome veneration for apparently marginal forms of plant and animal life and an almost fanatical determination to belittle any sense of mystery about human gestation." "I do believe that those who compare the religious Right to the Nazis have fallen victim to polemical heat prostration." As a theologian, he has set a high standard for anyone who wants to follow in his footsteps. As Msgr. George Rutler said of him, "Father Neuhaus did not hide his lamp under a bushel, and he did not wait passively for lamp stands to appear."

Richard John Neuhaus was born in Pembroke, Ontario, one of eight children to a Lutheran minister and his wife. He dropped out of school at fourteen and went to Texas where he operated a gas station. At this point in his life it was most unlikely that he would eventually be an adviser to popes and presidents. He never did receive a high school diploma but earned his BA and MDiv at Concordia Seminary in St. Louis, Missouri.

As an ordained Lutheran minister, he served as pastor from 1961–1978 to a predominantly black and Hispanic congregation at St. John the Evangelist Church in Brooklyn. He preached civil rights and social justice concerns from the pulpit. In his 1971 book *In Defense of People*, he castigated the ecology movement that placed "the rights of nature" above "the rights of man." While rejecting the notion that "Man is the measure of all things," he argued that "it is a thousand times preferable" to "Nature is the measure of all things."

Neuhaus's liberal views on politics and abortion underwent a radical overhauling with the arrival of *Roe v. Wade*. It greatly saddened him that so many of his colleagues who had ardently supported civil rights causes did not extend their humanitarian sympathies to the unborn. He knew, from analyzing polling data, that blacks were disproportionately opposed to abortion. He also knew that abortion deflected energy from solving the problems of poverty. Margaret Sanger, founder of Planned Parenthood, promoted forced sterilization for certain categories of human beings. Viewing a photograph of her addressing a Ku Klux Klan rally in the 1920s only confirmed Neuhaus's suspicion that the abortion movement contained a racist element.

As a defender of the rights of the unborn and the elderly, Pastor Neuhaus was both eloquent and forceful. In a presentation he made the year before he died, to the annual convention of the Right to Life Committee, he proclaimed:

"We shall not weary, we shall not rest, as we stand at the entrance gates and the exit gates of life, and at every step along the way of life, bearing witness in word and deed to the dignity of the human person—of every human person." Alas, Winston Churchill could not have said it any better.

Richard John Neuhaus was received in the Catholic Church on September 8, 1990, the Nativity of our Lady. A year later he was ordained a priest of the Archdiocese of New York by Cardinal O'Connor. As a priest, he continued to serve as editor in chief of the journal he founded: *First Things: A Monthly Journal of Religion, Culture and Public Life.* "The first thing to say about politics," Neuhaus once said, "is that politics is not the first thing." *First Things* gained the reputation of being the most influential journal of religion and public life. It conveyed, through a galaxy of scholars, that the moral strength of democracy is dependent on moral values and that Christian churches have a vital role to play in the flourishing of democracy. Father Neuhaus stressed the point, in his best-known book *The Naked Public Square,* that democracy in America should not be stripped of religious morality.[26] "Politics is chiefly a function of culture," he wrote, and "at the heart of culture is morality, and at the heart of morality is religion."

It has been said that Fr. Neuhaus underwent two conversions, one from liberalism to conservatism, the other from Lutheranism to Catholicism. Being the precise thinker that he was, he preferred to view his life in terms of a developing

---

[26] Richard John Neuhaus, *The Naked Public Square: Religion and Democracy in America* (Grand Rapids, Mich: W. B. Eerdmans Pub. Co., 1995).

story, a process of enlarging and maturing. In 1987, while he was still a Lutheran, he wrote *The Catholic Moment: The Paradox of the Church in the Postmodern World.*[27] Here, he expressed his personal conviction that "the Catholic Church is the leading and indispensable community in advancing the Christian movement in world history." He returned to this theme in a piece for *First Things* entitled "The Persistence of the Catholic Moment" (February 2003). He continued to see the Catholic Church as a unique and indispensable leader in furthering the Christian intellectual tradition, promoting the culture of life, and achieving Christian unity.

In "How I Became the Catholic I Was" (*First Things*, April 2002), he reiterated how his development, though a gain, was never a loss: "In the mystery of Christ and his Church nothing is lost, and the broken will be mended. If, as I am persuaded, my communion with Christ's Church is now the fuller, then it follows that my unity with all who are in Christ is now the stronger. We travel together still."

Fr. Neuhaus marched in Selma with Rev. Martin Luther King. He eschewed taking liberties with liberty and held to a liberalism that promoted the good of the community and the health of the individual. "All my life I have prayed to God," he once said, "that I should remain religiously orthodox, culturally conservative, politically liberal and economically pragmatic." Fr. Neuhaus has chartered a path for anyone who desires to live a life that is consistent, courageous, and truly Christian.

---

27   Richard John Neuhaus, *The Catholic Moment: The Paradox of the Church in the Postmodern World* (San Francisco: Harper & Row, 1987).

PART IV

Apostles From the World of Literature and Music

A MAN OF FAITH

Marshall McLuhan

Herbert Marshall McLuhan was born in Edmonton, Alberta in the year 1911. During his adolescent period, he explored his conflicted relationship with religion and turned to literature to "gratify his soul's hunger for truth and beauty." He later referred to this stage as agnosticism. While studying in England, he read G. K. Chesterton, whose effect on him was similar to the effect the latter had on C. S. Lewis. "A young man who wishes to remain a sound atheist cannot be too careful of his reading," Lewis remarked, after imbibing Chesterton's persuasive logic. McLuhan abandoned his agnosticism just as C. S. Lewis abandoned his atheism.

In a letter to his mother, in 1935, McLuhan revealed his indebtedness to the persuasive Chesterton: "Had I not encountered Chesterton, I would have remained an agnostic for many years at least." McLuhan completed his conversion process and entered the Catholic Church in 1937. His father accepted his son's conversion, but his mother was inconsolable and feared that his Catholic identity would hurt his career. This proved most emphatically not to be the case. In fact, McLuhan owed a great deal of his success to Catholic thinkers, especially to Saint Thomas Aquinas.

After teaching at the University of Wisconsin for a year, McLuhan taught at only Catholic schools: Saint Louis University, Assumption College, Fordham University, and St. Michael's College at the University of Toronto where he taught until 1979. He attended Mass on a daily basis. His approach to teaching was to help students sharpen their perceptions so that they could see exactly what was going on. He was a staunch enemy of propaganda and saw the media as propaganda's most effective ally. "The medium is the message" is his most popular aphorism and cuts to the essence of his thinking. Since the *medium* is the message, we must first understand the effect that radio, TV, newspaper print, movies, and other media forms have in distorting the message they convey. Without this understanding, the very medium hypnotizes us into unthinking servo-mechanisms. "All media exist," he maintained, "to invest our lives with artificial perceptions and arbitrary values." Not any of the fine arts, he argued, but "advertising is the greatest art form of the 20th century."

McLuhan's 1964 book *Understanding Media*[28] was a great success and was translated into more than twenty languages, although the subtlety of its message escaped many of its readers. It was required reading for aspirants to the presidency and earned its author the title of "Oracle of the

---

[28]   Marshall McLuhan, *Understanding Media: The Extensions of Man* (New York: Mcgraw-Hill, 1964).

Electric Age." Encomia were extravagant, regarding the work as "the most influential book by the most debated man of the decade." The *New York Herald Tribune* praised McLuhan to the level of "the most important thinker since Newton, Darwin, Freud, Einstein, and Pavlov."

McLuhan, however, was not bamboozled by media hype. He remained a man of deep faith and found it amusing that San Francisco hippies could applaud a Catholic whose thought was founded on the Thomistic notion that knowledge is an order of perceptions. McLuhan wanted people to stay "in touch."

I knew Marshall McLuhan personally and found him to be gracious, generous, and delightfully humorous. I once asked him why he had grown a moustache. "To obsolesce all previously existing photographs of me," was his instant reply. He wrote the foreword to my first book, *Abortion in Perspective.* Naturally, he was a defender of life and spoke at various pro-life conventions. He loved word play and there can be little doubt that his reference to the fact that diaper spelled backwards is "repaid" is associated with the infant care of his six children. The medium is the message, but it is also true that "the medium is the mess age" as well as the "massage," and that it is also the "mess sage," as well as the "mass sage." "All my words are on parole," he was fond of saying.

It has been said that McLuhan's greatest achievement was his fame. This is unfair to the perceptive student of the electric age. Personally, I am grateful to him for three things. First, is his serene confidence that the human mind is capable of understanding whatever it is that is unfolding within our electronic world. Here, the influence of Aquinas is apparent. As McLuhan stated again and again, "There is absolutely no inevitability as long as there is a willingness to contemplate what is happening."

The second is his personalism, his conviction that the whole person must be involved in order for understanding to take place. The specialist and the expert fragment things and therefore cannot see what is going on. "Comprehension," he writes, "is never mere classification. It means the perceiving of total processes by using every sense in any situation." He encouraged people to learn how poets could see things that escaped the more prosaic mind. Many of his aphorisms were provocative and got us to think more responsibly. "There are no passengers on spaceship earth. We are all crew." He was always ahead of his time, reminding us that the fate of the planet is in our hands.

Finally, I am indebted to McLuhan for his extensive treatment on the theme "breakdown is breakthrough." It is through our personal failures, our lack of unity with the world around us, that we can gain insights and see things we could not see if we were entirely one with the world. When our mores merge with the world, there is no self-consciousness. Thus, only the man who fails is eligible for success. McLuhan lived with the abiding faith that Christ's final breakdown—his crucifixion and death—preceded his ultimate breakthrough: the Resurrection.

I recall coming home after a New Year's Eve party and clicking on the TV. What I was told through this ubiquitous media form was that on the final day of 1979, communications expert Marshall McLuhan passed away. He seemed larger than life to me and I was stunned by the sad news. My prayers were laced with the hope that his final breakdown was his ultimate breakthrough.

Malcolm Muggeridge

One fine day in October of 1978, I boarded a train that would take me from Waterloo, Ontario to Toronto. A kindly looking lady shared my compartment. To facilitate conversation, she told me about her enthusiasm for the writings of Malcolm Muggeridge, regarded by many as one of the greatest journalists of the twentieth century. She could not have ventured a more appropriate opener. "I am on my way to an editorial meeting in Toronto where I will be speaking with the very same Malcolm Muggeridge," was, from her point of view, my surprising response. God-incidences like this must happen for a purpose. Here was "St. Mugg," as he was called, in full panoply, famous enough to endear himself to my co-traveler, humble enough to spend time with a struggling Catholic newspaper, and charismatic enough to establish a sympathetic bond between two strangers on a train.

Thomas Malcolm Muggeridge, known professionally as Malcolm Muggeridge, was born in 1903 in Sanderstead, Surrey, and the third of five sons. Throughout his life he saw himself as an instinctive disbeliever. He was so inclined to disbelieve practically everything he encountered that he found it difficult to believe almost anything. This was a personal trait that contributed to his success as a journalist and gave him an edge that endeared him to skeptics. But in the final analysis it was integrity, not skepticism, that proved to have a firmer hold on him.

At the beginning of 1933, Muggeridge made his way to the Ukraine to investigate reports of a famine. "I will never dare forget this," he wrote, "Farmers kneeling in the snow and begging for bread." It was through his reportage to *The Manchester Guardian* that the genocide in the Ukraine became well known. At the same time, a certain Walter Duranty, writing for *The New York Times,* denied the existence of the famine and, nonetheless, was awarded the Pulitzer Prize. Muggeridge had little regard for Duranty and called him "the greatest liar I have ever met in journalism." The whole experience left Muggeridge thoroughly disillusioned about communism in Russia and socialism in general. In 2008, on the seventy-fifth anniversary of the Ukrainian famine, Malcolm Muggeridge was awarded the Ukrainian Order of Freedom (posthumously) to honor his exceptional service to the country and its people.

In 1973 Muggeridge resigned as rector of the University of Edinburgh rather than approve students' request for a liberal distribution of "pot and pills." As rector, he expected his students to spearhead progress, produce outstanding works of art, and take their place as astute political leaders. Instead, Muggeridge saw them as degrading themselves with "the resort of any old, slobbering debauchee in the world at any time—Dope and Bed." Ironically, the two loudest voices that denounced his stance came from chaplains.

A more personal example of his integrity involved "the person I most loved in the world, my wife Kitty." Malcolm's wife was desperately ill, and her attending physician gave her only an outside chance of surviving. An emergency operation was necessary, but first, a blood transfusion was needed. At the very prospect that he could be the blood donor, "an incredible happiness amounting to ecstasy" surged up within her husband. His blood count was taken and found to be suitable. Malcolm and Kitty were then united through a simple glass tube with a pump in the middle. The health-giving blood began to flow from one to the other. "Don't stint yourself, take all you want," Muggeridge shouted to the doctor, as he perceived the immediate and salutary effect his gift had in restoring color to her face. It was the turning point; from that moment Kitty began to recover. Looking back on the incident, Muggeridge wrote: "At no point in our long relationship has there been a more ecstatic moment than when I thus saw my life-blood pouring into hers to revivify it." To give life is the purpose of love.

Conversion can be a long, convoluted process. Because of his integrity, Muggeridge was open to whatever was reasonable or beautiful. He loved the fine arts, and was inspired by the writings of Cardinal Newman, Shakespeare, Pascal, Tolstoy, Dostoevsky, Kierkegaard, and St. Augustine. He found the Gospels "irresistibly wonderful as they reduce the jostling egos of now—my own among them—to the feeble crackling flicker of burning sticks against a majestic sunset." How, except for divine intervention, could so loosely constructed narratives written in an ancient language, after so many centuries "still have the power to quell and dominate a restless, opinionated, over-exercised and under-nourished twentieth century mind?"

But it was his personal friendship with Mother Teresa that may have been the tipping point for is conversion. As he confessed in his final book, Conversion: A Spiritual Journey,[29] "Mother Teresa is, in herself, a living conversion: it is impossible to be with her, to listen to her, to observe what she is doing and how she is doing it, without being in some degree converted." There was no book he had ever read, no lecture he had ever heard, and no service he had ever attended "that has brought me nearer to Christ or made me more aware of what the Incarnation signifies for us and requires of us" than the living example of Mother Teresa.

Malcolm Muggeridge and his wife, Kitty, formally entered the Catholic Church on the twenty-seventh of November 1982, at the Chapel of Our Lady, Help of Christians in the Sussex village of Hurst Green. In attendance was a group of Down syndrome children who helped to make the occasion "an unforgettable experience." His entry into the Church gave him a sense of deep peace. In his own words, it was "a sense of homecoming, of picking up the threads of a lost life, of responding to a bell that had long been ringing, of taking a place at the table that had long been vacant."

Malcom Muggeridge passed away in November 1990 at his home in Robertsbridge, East Sussex, England at the age of eighty-seven.

---

29   Malcolm Muggeridge, Conversion: A Spiritual Journey (London: Collins, 1988).

G. K. Chesterton

Gilbert Keith Chesterton (1874–1936) was a child in many ways. He was a child of the universe, a child of nature, a child of wonder, and a child of God. But he was most certainly never a child of his age. An age is always narrow and one-sided. It has the infelicity of obstructing the timeless wonders of creation. "Every stone or flower is a hieroglyphic," he wrote, "of which we have lost the key." He was a man possessed with a vision that was enlarged by his faith. "The Catholic Church," he remarked, "is the only thing that saves a man from the degrading slavery of being a child of his age."

One of Chesterton's editors described him as having "the freshness and directness of the child's vision." Journalist William Oddie states that when he thinks of Chesterton, a phrase that constantly comes to mind is "whoever does not receive the kingdom of God like a little child shall not enter it." "All my mental doors open outwards into a world I have not made," he wrote. "My last door opens upon a world of sun and solid things. . . . The post in the garden; the thing I could neither create not expect . . . it is the Lord's doing and it is marvellous in our eyes."

Chesterton and his wife were unable to have children. Nonetheless, he gave a children's party every year from which adults were rigorously excluded. One excluded parent asked a child if Mr. Chesterton was really as clever as everyone said. "Oh yes," came the reply, "you should see him catching buns in his mouth."

Chesterton's writings are relevant to our age because they are equally relevant to all ages. "The Catholic Church, as the guardian of all values," he remarked, "guards also the value of words." And how Chesterton valued words, their meanings, their playfulness, and how they are windows to the world! "Fallacies do not cease to be fallacies because they become fashions." In so saying, Chesterton reminds us, however subtly, that the words *fashions* and *fallacies*, so similar in sound, can be light years away from each other in meaning. "It is not bigotry to be certain we are right; it is bigotry to be unable to imagine how we might have gone wrong." Here, G. K. offers courage to people who are right and know that they are right. After all, the importance of an open mind is its capacity to grasp the truth. On the other hand, he chastises those who lack the will to re-examine their own assumptions. He could be playful, profound, and philosophical in a single epigram: "Pride is the falsification of fact by the introduction of self."

To introduce G. K. Chesterton is to introduce him to his immense volume of writings. His life was free of both scandal and adventure. His words revealed his soul. And they were countless: more than four thousand articles, several biographies and an autobiography, the Father Brown detective series, several plays, two hundred short stories, approximately eighty books on a variety of topics, and several hundred poems. Regarding his book *Saint Thomas Aquinas: 'The Dumb Ox'*,[30] Thomistic scholar Etienne Gilson said, "I consider it as being without possible exception the best book ever written on St. Thomas Aquinas. Nothing short of genius can account for such an achievement." G. K. had the uncanny ability to write two distinct articles at the same time, one by hand while dictating the other to a secretary. His close friend Hilaire Belloc said of him that "his mind was oceanic. He swooped upon an idea like an eagle, tore it with active beak into its constituent parts and brought out the heart of it. If ever a man analyzed finally and conclusively Chesterton did so."

Concerning "Women's Liberation," Chesterton displayed both humor and insight: "Twenty million young women rose to their feet with the cry, 'we will not be dictated to,' and proceeded to become stenographers." Concerning the claim that child raising confines a woman to a small world, Chesterton questioned how it could be a large career to tell other people's children about arithmetic and a small career to tell one's own children about the universe. "How can it be broad," he asked, "to be the same thing to everyone, and narrow to be everything to someone? . . . I will pity Mrs. Jones for the hugeness of her task; I will never pity her for its smallness."

---

[30]   G. K. Chesterton and Dale Rogers, *Saint Thomas Aquinas, 'The Dumb Ox'* (San Francisco, CA: Ignatius Press, 1980).

Above all, Chesterton saw himself as a journalist. He wanted to bring his message directly to the ordinary citizen. He believed strongly in democracy and was not willing to deny a person his vote simply because of the accidental fact that he was no longer among the living. Therefore, he believed in tradition. He distrusted men who were clever and those who knew more and more about less and less. "When civilization wants a library cataloged, or the solar system discovered," he wrote, "or any trifle like that kind, it uses up its specialists. But when it wishes anything done that is really SERIOUS it collects 12 of the ordinary men standing about. The same thing was done, if I remember right, by the founder of Christianity."

Chesterton was adept at expressing a beautiful thought in a beautiful way. Two citations suffice to illustrate the point: "If seeds in the black earth can turn into such beautiful roses, what might not the heart of man become in its long journey toward the stars?" "The vow is to the man what the song is to the bird. . . . It is not easy to mention anything on which the enormous apparatus of human life can be said to depend. But if it depends on anything, it is on this frail cord, flung from the forgotten hills of yesterday to the invisible mountains of tomorrow."

G. K. Chesterton, by all accounts, was a man of exceptional charity. He was always able to see something good in opponents with whom he disagreed intellectually. For him, humanity was always more important than ideas. Some of his admirers have seen reason to begin pressing for this great writer and human being's canonization.

C. S. Lewis

On November 22, 1963, three towering figures of the twentieth century died. C. S. Lewis died in his brother's arms at 5:30 pm. One hour later, President John F. Kennedy was shot at 12:30 pm in Texas, and soon thereafter passed away. At 5:20 pm, local time, Aldous Huxley, author of *Brave New World,* surrendered his spirit just under eight hours after Lewis's demise. Lewis was a week shy of sixty-five; Kennedy was forty-six; Huxley was sixty-nine.

Peter Kreeft was taken by this coincidence and wrote *Between Heaven and Hell,* a dialogue in purgatory between these three men: Lewis, the Christian, Kennedy, the secular humanist, and Huxley, the Eastern pantheist. Could Lewis be as effective an apologist for Christianity in the next world as he was on earth? This imaginative piece of fiction brings to mind one of the central issues of life; namely, why the nearness of God can be recognized by some and remain irretrievably distant for others.

C. S. Lewis was, like the figure in Francis Thompson's

great poem *The Hound of Heaven,* consistently running away
from God: "I fled Him, down the nights and down the days;
I fled Him, down the arches of the years; I fled Him, down
the labyrinthine ways of my own mind." That flight, for
Lewis, however, was difficult to maintain. Hints of God's
reality were seemingly everywhere. God seemed to be "very
unscrupulous" in the various traps he set for the unbeliever.
"A young man who wishes to remain a sound Atheist," he
confessed, "cannot be too careful of his readings." For Lewis,
reading G. K. Chesterton was both inspirational and seduc-
tive. Yet, although God remained near, his existence for
Lewis remained but a shadow.

That "shadow" was Joy. But, on reflection, Lewis understood that Joy was something inward. To think about loving,
he mused, is to enjoy one's own thoughts. It is not "Contemplation," which moves outward toward something other
than the self. Joy, then, is merely a pointer to something far
more desirable than whatever sensations and images might
accompany it. In experiencing Joy, we are really experiencing
our yearning for God. If God exists, he cannot be a mere
part of my consciousness. He must have his own objective
reality.

Akin to the distinction between Joy and Contemplation,
for Lewis, is the distinction between life in its humdrum
quality and the richer life that we long for. The difference
between ordinary life and a more spiritualized life, he reasoned, is so great that different names should be assigned
to them. Therefore, he distinguished, borrowing from the
Greek, between *Bios* from *Zoe.* The former, *Bios,* is limited
and always tending to run down. It is a form of life that

is heading for death. However enjoyable it may be while it lasts, it cannot be completely satisfactory. The latter, *Zoe* or Spiritual life, comes from God and does not die. It is eternal. Lewis goes on to say that the difference between these two forms of life is as different as a photograph is from the reality it depicts, or a statue is from a real human being. Thus, as in the Pygmalion myth, changing from *Bios* to *Zoe* would be like changing from a piece of carved stone to an actual, breathing human being. "And that is precisely what Christianity is about," he concludes. "This world is a great sculptor's shop. We are the statues and there is a rumor going round the shop that some of us are some day going to come to life" (*Mere Christianity*, Book 4, Chapter 1). Becoming a Christian was like moving out of Shadowland.

In *Surprised by Joy*,[31] he offers a more personal and dramatic description of his conversion. He asks his reader to picture him alone in a room and feeling, night after night, "the steady unrelenting approach of Him whom I so earnestly desired not to meet. That which I feared had at last come upon me. In the Trinity Term of 1929 I gave in, and admitted that God was God, and knelt and prayed: perhaps the most dejected and reluctant convert in England. I did not see what is now the most shining and obvious thing; the Divine humility which will accept a convert on such terms."

God is ever near, though his presence is often blocked by the Spirit of the Times. Lewis knew that God would outlast whatever is temporary: "All that is not eternal is eternally out of date," he famously remarked. Thus, he decried what he

---

[31]   C. S. Lewis, *Surprised by Joy: The Shape of My Early Life* (2017).

called "Chronological Snobbery," the "uncritical acceptance of the intellectual climate of our own age and the assumption that whatever has gone out of date is on that account discredited." Like Mater Parrot, in his book *Pilgrim's Regress*, many people are mesmerized by the Spirit of the Times and simply parrot back the contemporary or politically correct answer to any question. The quest for God, then, requires a critical view of the present.

Lewis had read G. W. F. Hegel, F. H. Bradley, and other philosophers who posited a remote God that one could not meet. According to such thinkers, a person could no more meet God than Hamlet could meet Shakespeare. Lewis began reading the Gospel of St. John in Greek and ruminated about the significance of love. He had good and close friends who would meet on Tuesday mornings in a pub and on Thursday evenings in his apartment to discuss what each was writing at the time. This group of literary friends called themselves the Inklings and included Charles Williams, J. R. R. Tolkien, Owen Barfield, and other writers of note. Williams was his most admired friend. When he died, Lewis stated, "No event has so corroborated my faith in the next world as Williams did simply by dying. When the idea of death and the idea of Williams thus met in my mind, it was the idea of death that was changed." One meets God through love, since God is Love. And it is through that Love that one experiences eternal Life.

Whittaker Chambers

Whittaker Chambers, wrote Henry Regnery, who had known many great men during his long career as a publisher, was "one of the great men of our time." Chambers viewed himself in humbler terms as a man "tarnished by life" and yet "an involuntary witness to God's grace and to the fortifying power of faith." It was a life, nonetheless, that, for Regnery, "put all of us immeasurably in his debt." It was Chambers's unswerving conviction that "the crisis of the Western world exists to the degree in which it is indifferent to God." A defector from communism, Chambers described the vision of communism as "the vision of Man without God." And what he learned from godless communism allowed him to conclude that "Man without mysticism is a monster."

William F. Buckley regarded Chambers as "the most important American defector from Communism." It was because of Chambers's intimate involvement with Communism that he was able to expose Alger Hiss, former assistant to the Secretary of State and the golden boy of the liberal establishment, as a Soviet spy. From an historical perspective, this is how Whittaker Chambers will best be remembered.

The greatness of Chambers, however, if that term can be appropriated, was linked to something far less historical. It was his reverence for life, a virtue that he was slow to attain. The foreword to his best-selling autobiography, *Witness*,[32] is written in the form of a letter to his two children, urging them to appreciate "the wonder of life and the wonder of the universe" with "that reverence and awe that has died out of the modern world and been replaced by man's monkeylike amazement at the cleverness of his own inventive brain."

The notion of "reverence for life" in the popular mind is best associated with Albert Schweitzer for whom "ethics is nothing other than Reverence for Life. Reverence for Life affords me my fundamental principle of morality, namely, that good consists in maintaining, assisting and enhancing life, and to destroy, to harm or to hinder life is evil." For Dietrich and Alice von Hildebrand, "reverence is the mother of all virtues." Reverence is the realization that the wonders of life are not of one's own making, they ultimately reveal the Hand of God.

For the active Communist, however, there was neither time nor place for reverence for life. There was work to be done; the world had to be changed, as Karl Marx had insisted. It was expected, then, that high level communists would not have children. Unintentional pregnancies would be routinely aborted. As Chambers tersely states the matter, "There were

---

32 Whittaker Chambers, *Witness* (New York: Random House, 1952).

communist doctors who rendered the service for a small fee."
Yet the desire for life burned, however unconsciously, in the
soul of Whittaker Chambers. That same desire burned more
consciously and intensely in his wife, Esther.

She had conceived, and her pregnancy was confirmed.
Initially, they both agreed to have an abortion. But the realization that she was carrying a little human being gave her
pause. "Dear heart," she said to her husband, holding his
hands and bursting into tears, "we couldn't do that awful
thing to a little baby, not to a little baby, dear heart." On
hearing these pleading words, "the communist Party and its
theories, the wars and revolutions of the 20th century, crum-
bled at the touch of a child." As he confessed in his autobiography, "If the points on the long course of my break
with Communism could be retraced that is probably one
of them—not at the level of the conscious mind, but at the
level of unconscious life." Life has the innate power to oblit-
erate abstractions. And Communism was built on abstractions and was ripe to fall apart like a house of cards.

They had the child they yearned for who, "even before her
birth, had begun, invisibly, to lead us out of that darkness,
which we could not even realize, toward that light, which
we could not even see." They named the child Ellen and she
continued to lead her parents closer toward that light.

Ellen became "the most miraculous thing that had ever
happened in my life," as Chambers proudly asserted. One
day, while his daughter was sitting in her high chair and
smearing porridge over her face, his eye came to rest on the
delicate convolutions of her ear. In that meditative moment
the thought passed through his mind: "No, those ears were

not created by any chance coming together of atoms in nature (the Communist view). They could have been created only by immense design. Those "intricate, perfect ears," that were the result of design, also implied a Designer, more commonly known as God. "At that moment," Chambers writes, "the finger of God was first laid upon my forehead."

It was a moment of contact with God, a moment that transcends a world of suffering. He had once tried to explain to his son John that Beethoven, in his Ninth Symphony, "reached for the hand of God, as God reaches for the hand of Adam in Michelangelo's vision of the Creation." He severed himself from Communism "slowly, reluctantly, in agony," and finally wed himself to Christianity. He became a Quaker.

Chambers worked at *Time* magazine from 1939 to 1948 where he held various writing and editorial positions. He was a senior editor at *National Review* from 1957 to 1959. President Ronald Reagan, a longtime admirer of Chambers's writing, awarded him the Medal of Freedom posthumously in 1984 for his contribution to "the century's epic struggle between freedom and totalitarianism." Whittaker Chambers, née Jay Vivian Chambers, died of a heart attack on July 9, 1961 on his three-hundred-acre farm in Westminster, Maryland at the age of sixty.

His autobiography, *Witness*, apart from its socio/political significance, is a poetic, philosophical, and personal defense of reverence for life. It is also a moving account of how a child in the womb can exert the power to move hearts and change minds. It also reminds us, in his words, that "a nation's life is about as long as its reverential memory."

Joaquín Rodrigo

My wife and I had greeted the New Year with friends and were driving home, listening to the radio. A classical music station was on and the announcer informed us that the most requested piece of music throughout the concluding year was Joaquín Rodrigo's *Concierto de Aranjuez* for guitar and orchestra. This tidbit of news did not surprise me for, in the words of one esteemed musicologist, this work "has become, quite simply, the most successful concerto written for any instrument in [the twentieth century]." I recalled a previous hearing of the *Concierto*, this time not while my wife and I were riding in a car, but when we were sitting together in a theater and hearing it live.

That night, during the intermission, I had the distinct pleasure of speaking with the symphony orchestra's principal cellist, a devout family man, as well as a fine musician. The next piece on the docket was Joaquín Rodrigo's *Concierto de Aranjuez*, the first orchestral work composed specifically for guitar. I mentioned that the composer's profound grief over the loss of his unborn child provided inspiration for this work. My friend, a pro-life Catholic, was not aware of this, but seemed to be moved, and promised he would be thinking about it as he played the cello part.

The second movement, the *Adagio*, is chiefly responsible for this concerto's immense and enduring popularity. It is built on a three-note figure which is as persistent and arresting as the four-note figure that Beethoven employs in the first movement of his Fifth Symphony. It suggests a grief that will not go away. At the same time, its haunting beauty conveys a hope that will not die. The English Horn, well-known for its melancholy sound, opens the movement with a melody of nearly heart-breaking temper. There are echoes between the guitar and various instruments in the orchestra that could easily suggest the broken relationship between a father and his lost child.

Joaquín and his wife, Veronica, a brilliant pianist in her own right, remained silent for many years about the inspiration for the second movement. And so, the popular belief grew that it was inspired by the bombing of Guernica in 1937. In her autobiography, Victoria revealed that the inspiration was both an evocation of the happy days of their honeymoon as well as a response to Rodrigo's devastation at the miscarriage of her first pregnancy.

Rodrigo was born on St. Cecelia's Day in Sagunto, Spain on November 22, 1901. Cecelia was the name he gave to his daughter, after the Patron Saint of Music. Rodrigo was the youngest of ten children. At three years of age, he was seriously blinded by diphtheria. Medical treatment did little to improve his condition, and when glaucoma struck, his blindness became complete and permanent. Nonetheless, he did not allow regret to affect him and maintained that his blindness led him to music.

His musical gifts were most exceptional. By the age of eight he was studying piano and the violin in Braille. By the 1920s he had become a first-class pianist, capable of performing difficult works of Ravel, Stravinsky, and others. It is remarkable that although Rodrigo was an excellent pianist, he did not play the guitar. Nonetheless, he still managed to capture and project the role of the guitar in Spanish music.

He composed *Concierto de Aranjuez* in 1939, a time when the Spanish Civil War was ending and the Second World War was beginning. After its premier in Madrid, Rodrigo was borne shoulder-high around the city. Its huge success solved many of the financial difficulties that had plagued him and his wife. It also established his reputation as one of the most significant Spanish composers of the twentieth century.

Rodrigo was raised to Spanish nobility in 1991 by King Juan Carlos I. He died on July 6, 1999, having lived more than ninety-seven years, nearly the entire span of the twentieth century. He composed in Braille, and his output consisted of more than two hundred works, including eleven concertos, a ballet, an opera, background music for the cinema, as well as music for piano, voice, and full orchestra. Critics view his music in general as blending a vital, lyric happiness with strong touches of melancholy.

Rodrigo's compatriot and friend, Andres Segovia, one of the world's foremost guitarists, once said that "music is like the ocean and the instruments are little or bigger islands, very beautiful for the flowers and trees."

If music is like an ocean, it is because the human soul is also like an ocean, larger and deeper than any of the particular expressions that arise from it. And also, like the ocean, the human soul is unconquerable. The *Adagio* rises above adversity as it transmutes grief into hope. The surrounding circumstances of its creation are worth reiterating. Rodrigo's homeland was wracked by civil war. Europe was beginning to fall apart. Rodrigo and his Jewish wife were in exile, suffering from hardships of many kinds. There was the continuing blindness and the loss of his first child. Yet these were threads that were woven into hope. The noble melancholy of the *Adagio's* main theme becomes an expression of hope, an indication of the human soul's capacity to transcend an array of trials and tribulations that seem to be utterly devastating.

In her sonnet "On Hearing a Symphony by Beethoven," American poet Edna St. Vincent Millay writes:

> This moment is the best the world can give;
> The tranquil blossom on the tortured stem.

We need great music to remind us, if not to teach us, of the greatness of the human spirit. In times of difficulties, not to underestimate the work of God's grace, the soul can provide hope. The "tortured stem" is not our ultimate abode. Our destiny is to experience and enjoy the "tranquil blossom." Rodrigo once said, "I have observed that people who are moved by music are more sensitive to all manifestations of life." Music, indeed, is a vibrant expression of the life of the soul. Through music, we not only experience life but understand its communal nature. And like goodness, which, according to Saint Thomas Aquinas, spreads itself by its very own nature (*bonum est diffusivum sui*), music possesses this same Divine quality.

Alan Keyes

Alan Keys is a splendid example of integrating oratorical skill with philosophical soundness. If we are looking for an inspiring role model, one who integrates justice for both the unborn and for blacks, Alan Keyes is a most worthy choice.

Alan Keyes, born August 7, 1950, in a naval hospital on Long Island, New York, is a political activist who ran unsuccessfully for the presidency in 1996, 2000, and 2008. He became well-known to conservative African-Americans in the 1990s with his radio talk show *The Alan Keyes Show.*

Alan was educated at Cornell University, where he studied social political philosophy and was mentored by Allan Bloom. He subsequently earned a doctorate in governmental affairs from Harvard University. His dissertation, written under the guidance of Harvey Mansfield, was on Alexander Hamilton and constitutional theory.

He served under President Ronald Reagan as the American ambassador to the UN Economic and Social Council.

As a diplomat in the US Foreign Service, he served at the US Consulate in Mumbai, India, and later in the American Embassy in Zimbabwe. He is a devout Catholic and a third-degree Knight of Columbus. His wife, Jocelyn, is of East Indian descent from Kolkata. The couple have three children.

As a speaker, he is peerless. David Boldt, writing for *The Baltimore Sun* (Nov. 29, 1995), stated, "A Keyes speech on the moral erosion of America is one of those transcendent experiences where you just have to be there. It's hard to explain how he touches the soul of an audience and saying that he's 'silver-tongued' (as everyone does) only tarnishes the picture by inadequacy."

Cicero, who knew something about oratory, once said, "Orators are most vehement when they have the weakest cause, as men get on horseback when they cannot walk." Such is not the case with Keyes, who is an unusual combination of Demosthenes and Thomas Aquinas. And what he has to say is urgent, critical, and fundamental. "You can't have it both ways," as Keyes declares. "Either our rights come from God, as our Declaration of Independence says, or they come from human choice. If they come from human choice, then our whole way of life is meaningless; it has no foundation." In America, of course, human choice has been elevated to an unbarterable principle. The rationalization for abortion is founded on mere choice and nothing more exalted or anything more contextual. Therefore, Keyes can ask, "How does it secure the blessings of liberty to our posterity, to those generations yet unborn, to kill them, aborting them in the womb?"

Keyes's frankness seems shocking in a culture where people are "offended" by virtually anything. (Hans Christian Andersen's story of the "Princess and the Pea" comes to mind.) For example, certain health professions warn against using the expression "drug abuse." They advise "substance-use disorder" to avoid what they call "words that wound." "Attempted suicide" is now deemed unacceptable. "Unsuccessful suicide" is to be preferred.

In a culture of such hyper-delicate sensibility, how can abortion be discussed independently of its camouflaging euphemisms? Keyes does not fear to tread into regions deemed politically incorrect. Therefore, he is not reticent about the evil of abortion: "I frankly don't care if you agree with my stand on abortion. I take that stand because no other stand is consistent with decent principles, and no other standard is consistent with the will of God."

Keyes is appalled by the fact that although black Americans "make up 10 percent or 11 percent of the population," they account for "something of 40 percent to 45 percent of all abortions." There is a racist element in abortion that few people are willing to acknowledge.

Keyes and President Barack Obama clashed during their senatorial and presidential campaigns, though the latter was not insensitive to his opponent's gifts. "There was no doubt that the man could talk," the former president Obama noted in his book *The Audacity of Hope*: "At the drop of a hat, Mr. Keyes could deliver a grammatically flawless disquisition on virtually any topic." Obama, however, objected to the emotional intensity of his adversary. Despite his admiration for Keyes's oratorical skills, Obama confessed, "I found him getting under my skin in a way that few people ever have. When our paths crossed during the campaign, I often had to suppress the rather uncharitable urge either to taunt him or wring his neck."[33]

Keyes and Obama were polls apart electorally and poles apart personally. To me, however, when I conversed with Keyes, I found him to be mild-mannered, cordial, and generous. But behind a microphone, there was no one who could match him. Wherever he spoke, he owned the room. At the same time, Keyes had little affection for Obama's political ambitions. "Obama is a radical communist," he stated, "and I think that is becoming clear. That is what I told the people in Illinois, and now everybody realizes it is coming true. He is going to destroy this country, and we are either going to stop him or the United States of America is going to cease to exist."[34]

Nor did he approve of Obama's inclination toward judicial activism. "There is a difference between constitutional and judicial dictatorship," he maintained. "And I think it's time we remembered that our Constitution was not put together in order to establish the sovereignty of the judges. It was framed in order to guarantee the sovereignty of the people."

In May 2009, Alan Keyes, together with twenty-one others, was arrested while protesting Obama's commencement

---

[33]   Barack Obama, *The Audacity of Hope: Thoughts on Reclaiming the American Dream* (New York: Crown Publishers, 2006), p. 211.

[34]   Michael O'Brien, "Keyes: Obama an 'Abomination,' 'Radical Communist,'" The Hill, February 2, 2009, http://thehill.com/blogs/blog-briefing-room/news/campaigns/administration/38511-keyes-obama-an-abomination-radical-communist.

speech at the University of Notre Dame because of the president's support of abortion. He was charged with trespassing and released on a $250 bond. Being clearly, convincingly, and courageously pro-life has its perils.

If Alan Keyes's temperament and boldness made him at times unsuitable for politics, this may be a judgment against the present status of US politics. Nonetheless, Keyes's scholarship and keen sense of what is at the origin of things qualifies him as an important American figure. Drawing from his Harvard thesis, he has a most important message for his beloved country: "The moral principles of the Declaration of Independence, and the moral character required to sustain them, are the bedrock foundations of American liberty. Politicians who disregard these essentials in order to win votes may pose as the champion of this or that individual right, but as Hamilton observes in the Federalist #1, they are likely to be among 'those . . . who have overturned the liberties of republics . . . commencing demagogues, and ending tyrants.'"

We can all be passionate without apology when it comes to opposing demagogues and tyrants.

Ben Stein

In addition to handing out Oscars for acting, Hollywood should also be handing out awards for not acting; that is, for having the courage in the real world (and not the reel world) to say what is right when society thinks it is wrong. Perhaps an award called "Socrates" would be appropriate. If it did, Ben Stein would certainly be a nominee for having the common sense to declare that "abortion is a violent killing of the most innocent of humans" (reprinted in *The Human Life Review*, Summer 1998, p. 98).

In a January 2017 interview with *Fox* anchor Neil Cavuto, Ben Stein cited the hypocrisy that is going on in Hollywood. "I've earned my living in the vineyards of Hollywood for the last forty years," he said. "In that time, he came to realize that Hollywood is full of 'thuggish bullies.'" Although he did not indict all the citizens of "Tinsel Town," he affirmed that many of its celebrities act as "a united blacklisting front who will go against anyone that they think is politically undesirable." "To tell you the truth," he said, "it hurt me a lot, when my career was at its peak, when I was for example pro-life, that word got around that I was pro-life, and it hurt me a lot." It is sadly ironic that Hollywood liberals who are unsparingly critical of the blacklisting of actors that took place during the 1940s and '50s, now welcome what they formerly denounced.

Stein, fortunately, is honored outside of Hollywood. Bound4Life, a pro-life/pro-adoption organization dedicated to prayer, made Ben Stein its "Pro-life Celebrity" for 2009. In making the award, it formally recognized that "Mr. Stein has been a clear and active voice in the pro-life cause. He has used his gifts and platform in acting, writing, and speaking to present the truth of human-hood without compromise." The double meaning of the word *bound* is significant, referring to pro-lifers being journey-bound, and yet bound and gagged by the pro-abortion establishment. In 2003, the National Right to Life Educational Trust Fund, gave him its annual Pro-Life Award which is probably dearer to his heart than the Emmy he won for his TV series "Win Ben Stein's Money."

The multi-talented Ben Stein is an author, commentator, lawyer, teacher, actor, voice actor, humorist, game show host, comedian, screenwriter, speechwriter, producer, consultant, and if that is not enough, a composer. He was a speech writer for Richard Nixon and Gerald Ford.

Benjamin Jeremy Stein was born in Washington, DC on November 25, 1944. He graduated from Columbia University with honors, majoring in economics, and graduated as valedictorian from Yale Law School in 1970. He was a poverty lawyer in New Haven, Connecticut and then a trial lawyer for the Federal Trade Commission.

Despite his many triumphs, one success that stands out above all others is his fatherhood, which is the subject of his book *Tommy and Me: The Making of a Dad.*[35] After trying to have their own children, Ben and his wife, Alexandra Denman, decided to adopt. Ben was slow at first both comprehending and enjoying his new role as a father. Things changed dramatically one night after he told his son a bedtime story. "Well, good night, Tommy," he said to his son. And then his two-and-a-half-year-old son said, with perfect pitch and punctuation, "Good night, daddy." For poppa Stein, as he told CNN's Bobbie Battista, "It was the sweetest voice I've ever heard. And I was simply putty in his hands from then on. There's nothing that I would not have done for him, or wouldn't do for him after that." When people on business shows ask economist Ben Stein about a good investment, he always says, "The good investment is to go home from work early and spend the afternoon throwing a ball around with your son. That's a really good investment. The returns on it are tax-free. There's no possibility that you'll lose on it. And your son will reap enormous benefits from it."

One day, while Ben was cleaning out his son's room, a chore not usually associated with a celebrity, he happened to catch a TV talk show in which people were gushing over the presumed fact that we are now living in a "Golden Age." The S&P had tripled, and the S&P 500 had doubled over

---

[35]   Benjamin Stein, *Tommy & Me: The Making of a Dad* (New York: Free Press, 1998).

a relatively short period of time! More Americans are millionaires than ever before, *et cetera*. Stein was not enthralled. His thoughts turned to another set of numbers: "Last year, the Golden Age year of 1997, saw abortion 'clinics' and hospitals end the lives of about 1.4 million American babies" ("Ben Stein's Diary," *American Spectator*, May 1998). He thought of his son and how he "might have been sucked out and ground up in a 'clinic' or 'women's health centers' (most absurd terms for killing rooms for little girls and boys), before we learned what everybody now knows about just how alive a baby in the womb is." No matter how healthy the market is, it does not produce a Golden Age when so many innocent, human lives are prematurely extinguished by abortion.

For Ben Stein, being pro-life is hardly limiting oneself to a "single issue." "I would not be on any other side," he states, "than the side I'm on." And this is because, as he understands it, it is "pro-woman," saving millions of women from disgrace and disease; "pro-man" because it spares men from humiliation and disaster; and "pro-freedom" for it grants the child in the womb the freedom to be born. Furthermore, as he goes on to state, "If you value life when it's unborn, you set a standard for valuing life and for giving dignity to life that will stick with you and the society forever."

Life is broad and all-encompassing. Withdrawing the right to life of some is the beginning of withdrawing the right to life of others. Being pro-life is the thread that holds together the tapestry of all human life. We can thank Ben Stein for his courage and his common sense.

PART V

Apostles From the World of
Sports and Entertainment

James Connolly

"The times are never so bad," said Saint Thomas More, "that a good man can't live in them." These are encouraging words that can be applied to our present times. In addition to encouraging words, however, good people, especially Catholics these days, need heroes, people who beat the odds and offer hope for the many who feel they have little chance of succeeding.

One such hero, most worthy of introduction, is James Brendan Connolly (Irish: Séamas Breandán Ó Conghaile), one of twelve children born to poor Irish immigrants in South Boston. He developed his prowess as an athlete in the streets and vacant lots, where he joined other young men in running, jumping, and playing ball. He did not attend high school but was sufficiently self-educated that he was able to pass Harvard's entrance examination. As a result, he was unconditionally accepted at that school to study the classics.

It was 1896, the year the Olympic Games were being revived. The motto, *citius, altius, fortius*— meaning "swifter," "higher," "stronger,"—coined by Father Henri Didon, urged athletes to be at their best. This Dominican priest had envisioned the games as a means of using a physical competition to achieve spiritual greatness. "You who wish to surpass yourself, fashion your body and spirit to discover the best of yourself," he is reputed to have said.

James Brendan Connolly was a freshman at Harvard that year and possessed a strong desire to compete in the first of the modern Olympiads. He approached the dean of the college requesting permission to leave school in order to go to Athens but was refused. Connolly was one of the few Catholics attending Harvard at that time. He eschewed the safe and convenient choice of remaining at Harvard, getting his degree, and then making his mark in the world. Little did he know what immediate difficulties lay in store for him.

He had saved $250, but the German freighter which would take him and the nine other American athletes to Greece, suddenly raised the fare an additional $75. Through the intercession of Father O'Callaghan, himself a sports fan, parishioners raised the additional amount. The team planned to spend twelve days in training prior to the opening of the games. What was not known at the time was that Greece operated on the Julian calendar, which gave the ten athletes but one day to prepare. There were more problems. Arriving in Naples, Connolly's wallet was stolen. He almost lost his ticket, retrieving it after a pursuit of the robber.

On April 6, 1896, at 2 pm, the Modern Olympics got under way. Crown Prince Constantine of Greece made a speech, and King George I officially opened the games. James Brendan Connolly entered the first event, the triple jump, or more accurately, at that time, the "hop, hop and jump." He was the last of the competitors to compete in this event, and he out-distanced all his predecessors. With a jump of 13.71 meters—or 44 feet 11.75 inches, a remarkable 3 feet and 3 inches ahead of his nearest rival—he won the first championship of the modern Olympics and the first for his country. He became the first such champion since an Armenian prince by the name of Barasdates triumphed in boxing in the fourth century. Connolly was the first Olympic winner in 1,500 years—but received only a silver medal. The tradition of awarding gold to the winner was not inaugurated until 1908 at the London Olympiad.

Connolly also finished second in the high jump and third in the long jump. Some forty thousand spectators watched the events, including sailors from the USS *San Francisco*. In all, 285 men participated in the forty-two events, representing thirteen nations. Connolly watched with pride as the American flag was ceremoniously hoisted and a two-hundred-piece band played the *Star-Spangled Banner*. Jim Connolly returned home virtually penniless. He was by no means, at that time, a national hero. But the hero's welcome he did receive, from the Irish community of South Boston, made him feel like a king. He participated in the Paris Olympiad in 1900 and won a silver medal in the triple jump. He attended the 1904 Olympics as a journalist. "Connollystrasse" in Munich is named in his honor and was a key location in the events surrounding the Munich Massacre at the 1972 Summer Olympics.

Recognizing the merits of its former student and in an attempt to offset an infelicitous and hastily made decision,

the Dean of Harvard offered Connolly an honorary doctorate. Connolly, ever the man of integrity, refused it. He went
on to become a noted journalist and war correspondent. He
covered the Spanish American War, World War I, and the
Irish War of Independence. He authored twenty-five novels,
including *An Olympic Victor: A Story of the Modern Games*,
and two hundred short stories.[36] Joseph Conrad, himself an
accomplished teller of sailing adventures, once described
Connolly as "America's best writer of sea stories." He continued his distinguished and varied career until his death
on January 20, 1957, at eighty-seven. A collection of items
related to Connolly, including his triple jump silver medal,
is housed in the library of Colby College in Maine. A statue
in his honor stands in South Boston.

James Connolly beat the odds on so many levels. He was
the son of a poor family of twelve, growing up in a poor
area, bereft of a high-school education, and penniless at the
age of twenty-seven. Yet he became the first champion of
the Modern Olympic Games, a successful journalist, and
an accomplished novelist. Life, like the blade of grass that
breaks through the asphalt road, has a powerful potential
for asserting itself. We need role models such as James Connolly to remind us of this important fact. Life is an energy
which, when allowed its expression, leads us on to surprising
accomplishments. "The energy of the mind," wrote Aristotle,
"is the essence of life." The power that mind has over matter is something we often underestimate when our material

---

[36]   James B. Connolly and J. André Castaigne, *An Olympic Victor: A
Story of the Modern Games* (New York: Charles Scribner's Sons,
1908).

situation appears unhopeful. To be pro-life, however, also means to promote the life-energies that are stored in the reservoirs of the mind.

Mother Angelica

Three characteristics of a holy person, for some people, are sourness, self-righteousness, and aloofness. After all, according to this misconception, a person close to God must be far from mere humans. I think it is closer to the mark to say that what characterizes a holy person is jollity, humility, and accessibility. It is fun to be in the presence of a holy person. And I certainly found the company of Mother Angelica to be great fun. She had that special gift of inviting people (and God) into her life. Therefore, after listening to her deliver an engaging homily, I felt comfortable in saying to her, "You have told us that being a Christian is like being a tennis player: when you serve, you have an advantage."

When I met her in Vancouver, I apologized to her on behalf of the Canadian bishops who blocked the EWTN signal from coming into their country (the vacant spot was subsequently filled by the Playboy channel). There was not a trace of anger in her response: "Well, it just wasn't the right time; but we have some people working on it." There was the humility. We had breakfast together the next morning, and in a most welcoming gesture, she waved her hand and said, "Come on down" (to her TV headquarters in Alabama). She was the furthest thing from being aloof.

Rita Antoinette Rizzo was born on April 20, 1923 in Canton, Ohio. Her parents divorced when she was six. Then, things went from bad to worse. An only child, Rita was recruited by her mother to help with a faltering dry-cleaning business. At eleven years of age, she drove a car, barely able to peer over the steering wheel, delivering clothes to patrons who, all too often, could not pay. Tragedy struck when her parish priest, who had been most helpful to Rita and her mother, was murdered by the Mafia. Rita suffered from severe stomach pains and was treated for her nervous condition. Her mother was chronically depressed. Rita performed poorly in high school and once stated that she was not interested in the capital of Ohio but whether her mother committed suicide that day. It was an adolescence that seemed to be nothing but a blind alley.

When she was nineteen, on the advice of Rhoda Wise, who was hailed as a mystic, she made a novena. On the final day of that nine-day period of prayer, January 18, 1943, she declared that her stomach pain and the abdominal lump that had caused it, had completely vanished. This experience gave her the certitude that God had worked a miracle and that he knew and loved her: "All I wanted to do after my healing was give myself to Jesus."

On November 8, 1945, Rita Rizzo was vested as a Poor Clare nun, receiving a new name, which her mother had chosen for her: "Sister Mary Angelica of the Annunciation."

She was on her way to becoming Mother Angelica. In 1961, she, together with her sisters, established a community in Irondale, Alabama. It was named Our Lady of the Angels Monastery.

In 1981, Mother Angelica, using merely her entrepreneurial instincts and $200, launched what would become the world's largest religious media empire in the garage of a Birmingham, Alabama, monastery. Thanks largely from viewer donations, Eternal Word Television Network grew rapidly in both viewership and influence. Today EWTN reaches in the neighborhood of 264 million households daily in over a hundred countries. In 1999, while visiting Columbia, Mother Angelica had a vision which told her to build a temple in honor of the Child Jesus. As a result of $48.6 million in private donations, she was able to open the Shrine of the Most Blessed Sacrament of in Hanceville, Alabama later that same year.

The details of the meteoric rise of EWTN and the guiding presence of the Hand of God are meticulously narrated in Raymond Arroyo's biography, *Mother Angelica: The Remarkable Story of a Nun, Her Nerve, and a Network of Miracles* (May 15, 2007), a work that has received high praise from such luminaries as Lee Iacocca, Tom Monaghan, Peggy Noonan, George Weigel, and James Caviezel.[37]

In the year 2001, Mother Angelica suffered her first stroke. She would suffer much until her eventual death on Easter Sunday, March 27, 2016. She embraced the meaning

---

[37]   Raymond Arroyo, *Mother Angelica: The Remarkable Story of a Nun, Her Nerve, and a Network of Miracles* (New York: Doubleday, 2007).

of suffering and welcomed its arrival from day to day: "We don't understand the awesomeness of living even one more day. . . . I told my sisters the other day, 'When I get really bad give me all the medicine I can take, all the tubes you can stuff down me. . . . I want to live. . . . Because I will have suffered one more day for the love of God.'"

Mother Angelica's manner of speaking was always simple and direct. Her aphorisms will continue to charm and inspire: "You see, God expects His people to do the ridiculous, so He can do the miraculous." "God wants you to be in the world but so different from the world that you will change it. Get cracking." "Boldness should be the eleventh commandment." But her more extended wisdom could be equally effective: "It is because Jesus suffered, and we unite our pain with His, that suffering changes and transforms us. Only in eternity shall we see the beauty of the soul, and only then shall we realize what great things were accomplished by interior suffering."

Her special trio of virtues—jollity, humility, and accessibility—were revisited in a conversation she had with one of her biographers (Dan O'Neill, *Mother Angelica: Her Life Story,* 1986).[38] "I'm just God's donkey pulling his load for a while," she said to him. And then, while laughing, she showed him two photographs. In one shot, she is handing a replica of her satellite dish to Pope John Paul II in the Vatican. In the second, she is chatting with President Ronald Reagan. "Just imagine that," she says with a smile. Indeed,

---

[38] Dan O'Neill, *Mother Angelica: Her Life Story* (Birmingham, AL: EWTN Catholic Publisher, 1992).

and as we imagine that, we realize all the more how God intervenes in our lives without according any priority to one's station in life.

LIFE AND LEVITY

Sam Levenson

Laughter lifts the spirit. This is why humor is called levity; it is when we laugh we come closest to levitation. We are, after all, light-hearted beings. Because we can laugh at our troubles means that we can transcend them. Laughter, then, as good medicine, brightens our days and lengthens our lives.

Sam Levenson, as his name might suggest, was an accomplished humorist. He lived by the maxim handed down to us by Joseph Addison: "I shall endeavor to enliven morality with wit and temper wit with morality." He spent the better part of his life collecting jokes and witticisms from every legitimate source available. He passed away in 1980 and may have been one of the last "clean" humorists to have had a prominent place in the media.

In his 1979 book *You Don't Have to Be in Who's Who to Know What's What*, he remarks that "people have laughed at everything, except . . ." He pauses here in midsentence because the single exception stops him in his tracks. Then, he writes, "There is virtually no humor on the subject of abortion." He leaves it to the reader to ponder why abortion is not a laughing matter. At the same time, he leaves more than a hint as to what his own convictions are.

Abortion is not something to be celebrated or honored. We do not write odes, sing hymns, or create monuments to abortion. It does not have a place alongside of commitments such as marriage, coronations, baptisms, confirmations, *bar mitzvahs*, graduations, and oaths of office. Such commitments confer a new identity on a person: a husband or wife; a king or a queen, et cetera. Abortion is not a commitment; it is a rejection of commitment. It is a denunciation of motherhood. It is willed death, and therefore, something that cannot be part of a humorist's repertoire.

Sam Levenson was the youngest of ten children. He refers to his mother as the woman in Proverbs 31 who is praised for being the "woman of valor, strength, and dignity, whose children rise up and call her blessed." He takes care to cite the *Sanhedrin* which declares that he who saves one life on earth will be credited in heaven as having saved the whole world. Levenson earned a BA from Brooklyn College and an MA from Columbia University. He has received a number of honorary doctorates and was declared teacher emeritus of the New York City Board of Education. He married Esther Levine, his childhood sweetheart. Their modest honeymoon involved a trip from Brooklyn to Manhattan via the subway. They have two children and several grandchildren.

Concerning abortion, he argues that it "terminates life at its conception." He goes on to say that since "life potential . . . even at its microscopic tiniest, is already irrevocably programmed for life by life . . . Who has the right to deny the right of potentiality carried to term?" Drawing from his Jewish background, he reminds his readers that "the ancient moral injunction is to choose life." We cannot underestimate the value to mankind of each life. And this is because, as he writes, "I believe that each newborn child arrives on earth with a message to deliver to mankind. Clenched in his little fist is some particle of yet unrevealed truth, some missing clue, which may solve the enigma of man's destiny."

Not surprisingly, he is not exactly a champion of contraception. "Fraternization without maternization," he states critically, "is now a social doctrine that has been tightly compressed into a pill, *the* pill." Nor is he exactly enamored with the notion of "planned parenthood": "Recreation must be kept from running over into procreation. The idea is to junk the cradle but keep the playpen."

We can laugh our troubles away, but abortion is so dark a reality that it is repressed more than it is addressed. People generally deal with the aftermath of abortion not by laughing about it but by denying what it is. But abortion is far more than a mere choice. It is an end, and its formidable character does not allow it to be a subject for levity. Life can be hilarious; death has no charm. Sam Levenson, however, was undaunted and found humor in a wide assortment of topics.

- Concerning frustration: We have learned to space our children. Ten feet apart is just about right.

- Concerning suspicion: Whenever Adam came home late at night, Eve counted his ribs.
- Concerning disappointment: Money isn't everything. For example, it isn't mine.
- Concerning fear: With so many funeral homes around, it is not safe to be alive.
- Unexpected double meanings: Our tongue sandwiches speak for themselves. Due to the gravediggers' strike, a skeleton crew will do the digging. My doctor never treated me; I always paid.
- Inverting reality: Our teenage children are homesick only when they are home. An atheist is a person who has no invisible means of support. Columbus was wrong; the world is not round, it is crooked.
- Irony: When you add to the truth, you subtract from it.
- Annoyance: The longest word in the world is: "And now a *word* from our sponsor."
- Poverty: I could be happy with my lot if I had a lot.
- Death: "Be an angel and let me drive," the wife said to her husband. He did, and he is.
- The Bible: God made Adam before Eve because he did not want any suggestions.
- Wisdom: Render unto Caesar that which is Caesar's and unto God that which is God's. But remember that which you render unto God is deductible.

We can laugh because we can rise above the many annoyances of life. We can laugh because we can have a broad perspective on life and realize that even when things go wrong, there is still hope that they will eventually go right. Abortion is not a subject for laughter because of its hopeless finality. The aborted child cannot come back to life.

Before his untimely death at age sixty-eight, the champion of the VUPs (very unimportant people) bequeathed to his grandchildren "a prayer for peace" which includes the following sentence: "I leave not everything I never had, but everything I had in my life time: a good family, respect for learning, compassion for my fellow man, and some four letter words for all occasions, words like help, give, care, feel, and love."

Bob Cousy

He was Mr. Basketball, the Houdini of the Hardwood. He was blessed with long arms and peripheral vision. These gifts, together with being ambidextrous and having extraordinary court sense, introduced a new blend of ball-handling and passing skills that revolutionized basketball. He guided Holy Cross College to a national championship in 1947 and the Boston Celtics to six National Basketball championships. He led the NBA in assists eight straight years and was voted to thirteen NBA All-Star games. He was the league's Most Valuable Player in 1957. His number fourteen jersey, hung from the rafters of the Boston Garden, reminds Celtic fans of a basketball player the likes of which will never be seen again.

His autobiography, published in 1963, is titled *Basketball is My Life.* There can be little doubt, however, that the title is an editor's inspiration, one that would serve the public interest. But the real Bob Cousy's life belonged not to basketball but to his wife, Missie, who, for sixty-three years, was his loving partner in marriage.

Bob Cousy, the son of poor French immigrants, married his high school sweetheart, raven-haired Marie Ritterbusch, six months after he graduated from the College of Holy Cross. While Cousy was transforming the game of basketball, Missie was raising two daughters and instilling in them a passion for civil rights and the peace movement. "Our marriage was somewhat contrary to convention," Cousy said in an interview. "Most couples have the most intensity in the beginning. But I was always working. So we had the best and most romantic part of our marriage at the end. We literally held hands for the last twenty years."

Missie was known to be quick-witted, beautiful, and kind. She found a role in the world of basketball in mentoring the new Celtics' wives, especially those of black players such as superstars Bill Russell and Jo Jo White. She was a Girl Scout leader and a gardener, and adept at discussing politics. Around the house, she applied her versatility to the faulty plumbing in the family's English Tudor.

During the last dozen years of their marriage, writes columnist Dianne Williamson, "when Missie slowly succumbed to the ravages of dementia, her husband ensured that the woman he called 'my bride' was always by his side as her mind wandered where he couldn't follow" (*Worcester Telegram & Gazette*, September 29, 2013). "She was leading a happy life," said Cousy. "It was part of the game plan." And who knew better about game plans than her husband? But what exactly was this "game plan"?

Each morning, he would lay out Missie's pills, the

newspaper, a fiber bar, and a banana. Then he would gently awaken his "bride" and lead her to the kitchen where she would read the newspaper. It would take two or three hours for her to get through the pages since she would underline each sentence in every story. She would ask her husband the same question over and over. She sometimes hallucinated, became disoriented, and struggled to retain her balance. But she always recognized her husband and bristled at any suggestion that she was suffering from dementia. Cousy did all the household chores while graciously letting her think that she did them herself. He even had her station wagon sent to their home in Florida each winter so that she could see it in the driveway and continue to believe that she could still drive.

On September 7, Bob and Missie went to an early dinner at the Worcester Country Club. On the way home and in the car, Missie suffered a massive stroke. She died peacefully two weeks later and was laid to rest in St. John's cemetery. Loved ones aver that Bob's grief left him "inconsolable."

When asked what he misses most about his wife, Cousy struggles for composure: "I can't put the pills out in the morning. And I can't care for her anymore." Nonetheless, each night, when he goes to bed, he tells his wife that he loves her. He never felt defeated by the challenge of caring for his ailing spouse on a full-time basis. "It drew us closer together," he said. "It was never a chore, because I knew she would have done the same for me."

As much as Bob Cousy was a hero on the court, he was a greater hero off the court. It may be that the most important feature of his fame as a basketball player was that it served as a megaphone to let the world know how loving and dedicated a husband can be and how marriage, for better or for worse, can strengthen with age and flourish even in the face of adversity. Mr. Basketball, still active, turned eighty-eight on August 8, 2016.

Samer Kalaf wrote an article for the *Worcester Telegram & Gazette* entitled "This Story about Bob Cousy Will Break Your Heart." With all due respect to the author, the story should *warm* the heart, in addition to deepening our respect for marriage. Bob Cousy may not have read any of the works of Jean Vanier, but he put in practice for his wife what Vanier did for others. Life is to be treasured, perhaps even more if the beloved is one's spouse.

The manner in which Cousy cared for his wife is an inspiration. It reminds us that all the while we live, *to care* is the most authentic way in which a person *can be*. According to a Roman myth, Care was amusing herself one day by molding earth in various shapes. Finding a particular shape that she wanted to have life, she beseeched Jupiter to grant it a soul. Jupiter obliged but objected when Care wanted the new creature to be named after her. Saturn, the god of Time intervened, ruling that upon death, the creature would return to earth, its soul to Jupiter, but all the Time it was alive it was to be entrusted to Care.

The Houdini of the Hardwood should be better known as the Custodian of Care.

Alec Guinness

Sir Alec Guinness (1914–2000), a convert to Catholicism, is best known to modern movie aficionados as Obi-Wan Kenobi, the Knight of the Jedi. Ironically, he almost turned down his memorable role in "Star Wars." Commenting on the film's benevolent power in the universe and the oft' repeated phrase "May the force be with you," Guinness said that as a Christian he does believe that something like the "force" exists, "But not as expressed in "Star Wars."

That "force"—that is, the grace of God—was surely with Sir Alec throughout his lifetime and was filtered through to him in the form of many friends whom he regarded as "Blessings in Disguise," also the title of his 1985 autobiography. Counted among his innumerable friends are Sir John Gielgud, Dame Edith Evans, Sir Ralph Richardson, Dame Edith Sitwell, Evelyn Waugh, Noel Coward, and Sir Laurence Olivier. He treasured his friends, as indicated by the closing line of his autobiography, "Of one thing I can boast; I am unaware of ever having lost a friend."

In 1945 he met Pius XII. "I felt for the first time in my life that I had met a saint," he later wrote. He also met Pope John XXIII and Pope Paul VI. He was among the pilgrims in St. Peter's Square in 1994 for the Easter morning Mass celebrating by Pope Saint John Paul II. "I decided," Guinness relates, "that his voice is the most beautiful and dignified speaking voice I have ever heard."

Boastfulness was not in the least characteristic of Sir Alec. Despite his great success on stage, screen, and television, he confessed that "he is not at all proud of his achievements and repelled by the limelight." With regard to acting, he saw himself as a mere "interpreter of other men's words." Although acting was the fulfillment of his adolescent dream, he longed for something more, something that revealed the wholeness of his personality.

Two tensions threaded their way through the life of Alec Guinness. One was personal, the other, historical. When he was asked to write his autobiography, he found the proposal most flattering to his "Ego" but appalling to the "I" that had to do the job and somehow make it a worthwhile enterprise. "Ego seems to have disappeared," he informs us. "But not for long, I know. I can hear his lightest tread." He was constantly trying to keep ahead of his demons, "Impatience, Fretfulness, Hurt-Pride, Laziness, Impetuosity, Fear-of-the-Future, and lurking nearby, Lack-of-Common sense."

The other tension was between history and the moment. For him, one of the most penetrating statements of G. K. Chesterton is that "the Church is the one thing that saves us from the degrading servitude of being a child of his own time." There was nothing terribly special about his entrance into the Catholic Church, "just a sense of history," he tells is, "and the fittingness of things. Something impossible to explain." As Père Teilhard de Chardin aptly expressed it, "The incommunicable part of us is the pasture of God." Who can explain what transpires in that unique moment of grace between man and God?

There were specific moments on the road to his conversion that are, perhaps, more palpable. In 1954 he was in France and playing the role of Fr. Brown in a movie released in the United States as "The Detective." On his way back to his lodging, dressed in clerical attire, a young boy of seven or eight came up to him, held his hand tightly, addressed him as "Mon Père," and kept up a non-stop prattle. Guinness did not dare speak to him "in case my excruciating French should scare him." Suddenly, with a "Bonsoir, mon père," and a bow, he disappeared through a hole in a hedge. Guinness reflected "that a Church which could inspire such confidence in a child, making its priests, even when unknown, so easily approachable could not be as scheming and creepy as so often made out. I began to shake off my long-taught, long-absorbed prejudices."

His son, Matthew, then eleven, was stricken with polio and paralysed from the waist down. The future for Matthew looked doubtful. After dropping into a little Catholic church several times, Guinness made a negative bargain with God. "Let him recover," he said, "and I will never put an obstacle in his way should he ever wish to become a Catholic." About three months later, Matthew was able to walk. Not too long after that, he could play football. At age fifteen, Matthew became a Catholic.

The time and circumstances surrounding his birth was something to escape from rather than something to perpetuate. He never knew his father, whose name was left blank on Alec's birth certificate. His mother was variously described in obituaries and biographies as a "part-time barmaid" and "prostitute." Alec had three different last names before he turned fifteen. When he set out to seek his fortune, he had but four pence in his pocket. The man who was destined to be knighted never forget his humble beginnings.

Guinness speaks of having "near-psychic experiences." The objective reader of *Blessings in Disguise* would no doubt rate them as genuine. One of these experiences would be of particular interest to fans of the cinema. It was the autumn of 1955. Sir Alec had arrived in Los Angeles to appear in his first Hollywood film, *The Swan*. While at a restaurant, "a fair young man in sweat-shirt and blue-jeans" came up to him. "My name is James Dean. I'd like to show you something," he said, bursting with pride. It was a sports-car, wrapped in cellophane and tied with ribbon. It had just been delivered and its new owner had not yet driven it. Guinness, rather than share the stranger's joy, "heard himself saying in a voice I could hardly recognize as my own, 'Please, never get in it.'" He looked at his watch. "'It is now ten o'clock, Friday the 23rd of September, 1955. If you get in that car you will be found dead in it by this same time next week.'" Returning to his normal voice, he apologised for what he had said. Nonetheless, at four o'clock in the afternoon of the following Friday, James Dean was dead, killed while driving his sports car.

Sir Alec Guinness was a most extraordinary person. He will be remembered mainly for his superb acting skills. But he was far more than that. He was a man of deep faith, unusual modesty, exceptional spiritual acumen, and a great love for life.

Mother Dolores Hart

"Stop and consider!" said John Keats. "Life is but a day; a fragile dew-drop on its perilous way from a tree's summit." We stop and consider the dangers to and the brevity of life. This consideration takes on even sharper focus in an age of abortion.

On October 15, 2016 Mother Dolores Hart spoke at the seventeenth annual Respect for Life Conference in Meriden, Connecticut. She told her audience of two hundred people that because of financial difficulties, her own mother considered aborting her. The aborted, she explained, are people "whose lives will be unmet." They are doomed never to be known by others and never to know anyone. From her own perspective, having been known by so many people and knowing so many herself, made her allusion to the tragedy of abortion all the more powerful. The potential good that one can do, but can never do because of abortion, leaves an unmeasurable void in the world.

Dolores Hart came into the world on October 20, 1938 in

Chicago, Illinois. She was the daughter of actor Bert Hicks and a niece of Mario Lanza. Important interconnections between those who were destined to know her and those whom she was destined to know may be a signature characteristic of her life. She was not born a Catholic but chose to enter the Church at the age of ten. After high school, she studied at Marymount College in California. Using the stage name Dolores Hart, she was given the role of Elvis Presley's love interest in the 1957 release *Loving You.*

As an actress, she was in frequent demand and starred in ten films. She had a multi-year contract with Metro Goldwyn Mayer and was earning $5,000 per week. But the relationship with Elvis Presley continued to be a top story with both the public and the press. Decades later, even when Mother Dolores was ensconced in a cloistered monastery, the question persisted: "What is it like to kiss Elvis Presley?" Not bereft of a sense of humor, she once replied, "I think the limit for a screen kiss back then was something like fifteen seconds. That one has lasted forty years."

Hollywood gossip can be both tasteless and merciless. One interviewer asked her if she had heard the rumors that Elvis left her pregnant and Col. Tom Parker forced her to get an abortion. In response, she said, while laughing, "It was preposterous because of all the men I ever worked with, Elvis and my relationship was the most fraternal." "I'd done two movies with Elvis Presley," she told the press. "I'd been around Hollywood for a while and saw how needlessly competitive and negative it could be. It never held my interest."

At age twenty-five, Dolores Hart broke off her marriage engagement, left Hollywood, and became a Roman Catholic nun in the Benedictine Abbey *Regina Laudis* in Bethlehem, Connecticut. Her fiancé, an architect by the name of Don Robinson, never married, but visited her at the abbey every Christmas and Easter until his death in 2011. She declared her love for him, but, as Don said, "Every love doesn't have to wind up at the altar."

Mother Dolores Hart saw all the incidents of her life as "a tapestry that God has designed." Part of this tapestry involved the well-known actress Patricia Neal. After her divorce, and out of desperation, Patricia went to France. There, by happenstance, she met Maria Cooper Janis, a devout Catholic and close friend of Mother Dolores. Patricia spilled her troubles to Maria who said to her, "I am going to send you somewhere where I know you are going to be helped." The "somewhere" was *Regina Laudis*. Through a long recovery at the abbey, and through the guidance of Mother Dolores, Patricia Neal wrote her autobiography, *As I Am*. Neal, who for some time expressed the desire to enter the Church, finally obtained her wish shortly before she died. She is buried on the grounds of the abbey.

Maria Cooper Janis is the wife of the world renowned concert pianist Byron Janis and the daughter of Gary Cooper. The latter, a friend of Mother Dolores, was baptized a Catholic in 1959. Gary Cooper died of cancer a year later at age sixty on May 13, the feast day of Our Lady of Fatima. His last public words, spoken nine days before he passed away, reflected the noble characters he portrayed on the screen, especially that of Lou Gehrig in *The Pride of the Yankees*: "I know that what is happening is God's will. I am not afraid of the future." This particular segment of the tapestry also involves Pope Pius XII, with regard to Gary Cooper and his wife, and Pope John XXIII with regard to Dolores Hart.

In 2006, after forty-three years in the monastery, Mother Dolores Hart traveled to Hollywood to raise awareness for idiopathic peripheral neuropathy, a neurological disorder that afflicts her as well as many Americans. In that same year, despite her condition, she testified at a Washington congressional hearing on the need for more research on this painful and crippling disease.

In 2013, Ignatius Press published Mother Hart's biography, *The Ear of the Heart*.[39] Raymond Arroyo, EWTN's news director, reviewed the book and was impressed by "how listening with the 'ear of the heart' she [Mother Dolores] heard God's call and dared to respond. Her journey powerfully demonstrates that we must be willing to lose our lives and forfeit our plans to discover our true purpose."

Mother Dolores Hart celebrated her Jubilee Year in 2016, fifty years of vowed life at *Regina Laudis*. As prioress, dean of education, together with sundry other hats she was pleased to wear, she served as the still-point in a moving world. A dew-drop may be small and fleeting, yet it can also be seen as forming a prism through which the lives of countless individuals are refracted and perhaps reformed. Her life's journey has not been perilous as much as it has been providential.

---

39   Dolores Hart, *Ear of the Heart* (San Francisco: Ignatius, 2018).

A Radical Priest for Life

Father Ted Colleton

What does it mean to be a "radical"? One might think of the sixties decade when hippies identified themselves in this manner. In addition, radicals are usually understood as people who have "leftist" views. Father Ted Colleton, CSSp. Was an orthodox Catholic priest and resolutely pro-life. Could he ever see himself as a radical? The question taunted him when a newspaper reporter asked him, "How do you feel about being considered a radical?" Like a good soccer player, he side-stepped the issue: "Most people who call us radicals do absolutely nothing themselves. It is merely a cop-out."

Later, alone in prayer. Fr. Ted put the question to himself: "Am I a radical?" Well, he thought, "radical" refers to the *root* whereas its opposite refers to the *surface*. Therefore, it is better to get at the root of an issue, than remain a superficial onlooker. "I don't mind being called 'stupid' or 'dumb' or 'ugly,'" he mused, "but I would hate to be considered shallow." Thus, was planted the inspiration for the titles of two of his three books: *Yes, I'm a Radical* (1987); *Yes, I'd Do It Again* (1990); and *I'm Still A Radical* (2001).[40]

Edward (Ted) Colleton was born and raised in Ireland. At the age of twenty-seven, he was ordained a Catholic priest in the Spiritan (Holy Ghost) order in 1940. The following year, he was assigned to Kenya, in East Africa, and spent thirty years there as a missionary until he was expelled by the dictator Jomo Kenyatta. The circumstances surrounding his deportation are worth noting since they reveal something of Fr. Ted's heroic character.

On one particular occasion, Kenyatta spoke disparagingly about the missionaries before a large gathering of people. It was clear that his speech was a gross insult to the various missionaries, Protestant as well as Catholic, who had been dedicated to the progress of the local people. After much mental turmoil, Fr. Ted dispatched a letter to Kenyatta which included the following words: "No doubt we missionaries made many mistakes in the past, but I do not think we deserve to be publicly insulted by the First Citizen of Kenya. May I remain, Your Excellency, Respectfully Yours . . ." The response was something other than what Fr. Ted had hoped for. He was given twelve hours to leave the country. His letter marked him as an "undesirable alien."

As he was about to be driven to the airport that would take him out of Africa, he found himself looking at the faces of about ten policemen and a few woman secretaries.

---

[40]   Ted Colleton, *Yes, I'm a Radical* (Toronto: Interim Publishing, 1987); Colleton, *Yes, I'd Do It Again* (Toronto: Interim Publishing, 1990); Colleton, *I'm Still a Radical* (Toronto: Interim Publishing, 2001).

Fr. Ted has never made a secret about his flair for the dramatic. When he was a high-schooler, he was equally at home in comedy, tragedy, and Gilbert and Sullivan musicals. In his senior year, he felt pulled in opposite directions. "Should he become an actor or a priest?" Facing his opponents, he braced himself for what may have been his finest hour: "Ladies and gentlemen. After thirty years in Kenya, I am leaving. I am taking with me my pajamas, a shaving set, and a Bible. I hope that everyone who comes to your country puts in as much and takes out as little. Good night."

From Kenya, it was off to Canada where he began a second career, this time as a pro-life missionary. In all his years in Kenya, he never heard of an abortion. He spoke two African languages—Kikuyu and Ki-Swahili—and did not know the word for abortion in either language. Babies were regarded as a gift from God. The notion of killing a baby, born or unborn, to avoid inconvenience, never entered the minds of any of the people he knew.

Having come from a place where pregnant women were honored and revered, Fr. Ted was shocked at what he found in Canada. "To find that a doctor could set up an illegal abortuary where babies are murdered every day and it is guarded by the 'Forces of Law and Order' twenty-four hours a day!" His new mission was to teach Canadians about the sacredness of life that his friends in the Third World had already known. Having ministered to those living in material poverty, Fr. Ted would spend the rest of his life ministering to the spiritual poverty of Canada. He would endure calumny, slander, persecution, and imprisonment. What was most unsettling for him was being heckled from the pew while saying Mass. Yet he remained ever kind and forgiving, though he was "thoroughly ashamed" of the abortion-promoting work of "Catholic" politicians.

Two months before he turned ninety, Fr. Ted sent me a letter thanking me for mailing him a copy of my book *The Heart of Virtue*.[41] Consistent with his concern for others, he had loaned it to a fellow priest who was recovering in hospital from a broken thigh. "He is more spiritual and intellectual than I am," he stated, in keeping with his modesty. He expressed the hope that we would meet again, soon. It was not in God's plan, however. I treasure his letter. It remains a permanent part of my memorabilia.

My memory of him is a happy one. He was a master after-dinner speaker and had audiences howling with laughter over his repertoire of jokes and anecdotes. I marvelled at his energy and his attempt, not always successful, to remember the names of everyone he had met. He enjoyed amusing children with an assortment of card and coin tricks. I always found him to be both cheerful and hopeful.

On her deathbed, Fr. Ted's mother whispered: "Edward, be a good priest." And that he was throughout his priestly tenure of seventy years. Fr. Ted passed away peacefully in 2011 at the age of ninety-seven, his last days spent in quiet prayer. He was lauded by Jim Hughes, Campaign Life Coalition President, as "one of the great heroes of the Canadian pro-life movement . . . giving everything he had for the unborn and vulnerable." *Natura il fece e poi ruppe la stampa* (nature made him and then broke the mould).

---

41   DeMarco, *The Heart of Virtue.*

Wellington Mara

An unexpected gift arrived in the mail some time ago—a copy of Judie Brown's autobiography, courtesy of Wellington Mara, co-owner of the New York Football Giants. It was on the basis of my friendship with Mrs. Brown and the fact that I was seen as "a co-worker in her mission to protect God's preborn children" that I became the beneficiary of his generosity. But I was also the beneficiary of his humility-inducing magnanimity. He was truly a giant of a man.

Wellington Timothy Mara was born in Rochester, New York on August 14, 1916, the youngest son of Tim Mara, who founded the New York Giants football team in 1925. That was the year Wellington entered the National Football League, though in the inglorious role of a ball boy. He became the co-owner of the Giants from 1959 until his death on October 25, 2005. During his tenure at the helm, he became one of the most influential and iconic figures in the history of the National Football League. He was enshrined in the Pro Football Hall of Fame in 1997 and elected to the New Jersey Hall of Fame in 2012.

Mara was highly respected by his players. When Lawrence Taylor (better known to football fans as LT) was inducted into the Pro Football Hall of Fame, he thanked Mara for supporting him during the worst times of his drug addiction, stating, "He probably cared more about me as a person than he really should have." Taylor credited the Giants' owner for helping him to turn his life around and live a clean life style.

Wellington Mara's pro-life work is well-known and he has urged businesses and professional organizations to use their "time, their talents, and their treasure" to promote respect for life. At the time of his passing, he was survived by his wife, Ann (1929–2015), eleven children, and forty-two grandchildren. It has been reported that his team honored him after his death by trouncing the Giant's biggest and oldest rival, the Washington Redskins, 36-0 on October 30, at Giants Stadium. When his name was mentioned, the crowd of eighty thousand gave him a standing ovation.

On April 21, 1999, the National Right to Life Educational Trust Fund hosted its sixth Proudly Pro-Life Awards dinner. The guest of honor that night was Wellington Mara. The occasion raised over $1 million to further the pro-life cause. Mara was reluctant at first to receive the award, but finally consented in the name of Life Athletes, a group he founded. Other winners of the award include Mother Teresa, Pope John Paul II, Knights of Columbus Supreme Knight Virgil Dechant, Rep. Chris Smith, and Mrs. Arthur DeMoss. "God blessed me with a long life," Mara said at the

dinner. "During that lifetime I have formed a clear percep-
tion of the absolute sanctity of life and the unshakable conviction that, of all God's gifts, it is the most precious—and
is becoming the most tenuous," he told the seven hundred
people in attendance. "We live in an age," he went on to say,
"when mankind, in its arrogance, seeks to abrogate to itself
the right to limit or deny life to the afflicted and the unborn.
That is the challenge of our generation. The challenge and
the shame." He looked to Life Athletes to provide critically
needed role models for America's youth.

Chris Godfrey, executive director of Life Athletes and
owner of a Super Bowl ring, thanked Mara for being a man
of exceptional integrity. "But more importantly," he said,
"I'd like to thank him for asking me to walk alongside of
him to build a culture of life, which, in the bigger picture, is
far more important than winning a Super Bowl." After the
Giants won Super Bowl XXI, defeating the Denver Broncos
in 1987, Mara called six players on the winning team to
put together a video, "Champions for Life," which sparked
the creation of Life Athletes. Included in the message the
athletes delivered is the importance of chastity. Masculinity
does not imply promiscuity.

Ben Stein, movie actor, law professor, television personality, presidential speech writer, and pro-life advocate served
as master of ceremonies of the event. "We are rightly concerned," he told the gathering, "about the thousands of innocent men, women, and children in villages far, far away with
names we cannot pronounce. But here at home, the same
government that is outraged at what's going on in Kosovo is
using every trick, every lie, every device possible to allow the

current ongoing killing of almost 1.4 million totally innocent American children every year in places with names we
know very well, like Los Angeles and Dallas and New York
and Miami."

Stein, who played the boring high school teacher in the
1986 comedy *Ferris Bueller's Day Off* is anything but boring
when it comes to the defense of innocent life. "For me, the
number one issue is right to life," he said. "The thing about
Hollywood people is they think of themselves as workers
and proletarians and the warriors of the revolution, but
they're also snobs. They're incredible snobs."

Monsignor George Rutler, a close friend of Mara, reminded
the world of the importance of Mara's legacy. Whether he
attended the funeral of Rutler's mother or a birthday party
for the monsignor, Mara was always "the archetypal Catholic gentleman distinguishing himself in his pro-life work,
very practically engaging football stars in his 'Athletes for
Life' which helped the moral formation of young boys in our
morally desolate culture."

Wellington Mara understood the permanent relevance of
Church teaching in a world that is constantly yielding to
passing fads. "The Church has never changed its teaching on
the sanctity of human life," he once said. "It didn't make up
a rule for the convenience of a particular time like a rule at a
country club as the Governor would have us believe."

Wellington Mara succumbed to lymphoma at the age
of eighty-nine. He is buried at Gate of Heaven Cemetery
in Hawthorne, New York. The *Seattle Times* had this to say
about his passing: "On a crisp autumn afternoon, perfect
for the game he loved, New York Giants owner Wellington

Mara was revered Friday as a peerless father, friend and football man at a service packed with luminaries." We may believe there were angels among the luminaries.

PART VI

Apostles From the World of Politics and the Arts

A MAN OF MAGNANIMITY

Bob Casey

St. Alphonsus Liguori makes the comment in his book *The Incarnation, Birth and Infancy of Jesus Christ* that Jesus was born "in poor ragged clothes, in a stable lying on straw in a manger for animals," because "he came to destroy the pride which had been the cause of man's ruin."

Because of their affection for St. Alphonsus Liguori, a certain Pennsylvania couple, devout in their Catholic faith, named their son after him. And the young Alphonsus Liguori Casey (1893–1956) learned about hardship and poverty at an early age. He was orphaned when he was eleven. In order to support his brothers and sisters, he went to work as a mule boy in the anthracite coal mines of Scranton, Pennsylvania. He labored during the day and studied at night pouring over his high school studies. A mine, a cave, or a manger is a good place to learn humility. Alphonsus never forgot the lessons he learned in his youth. He graduated from high school and in his thirties earned a law degree. He then set up a law practice representing miners in their claims against the company.

His son, Robert, achieved enough distinction in his life to justify writing an autobiography (*Fighting for Life*) in which he recalls his earliest memories of the scarred hands of his father. He revered the legacy that Alphonsus brought to him from the mines of Scranton that included a visceral identification with the weak and the vulnerable. It seemed perfectly logical in Robert's mind to extend the special empathy he learned from his father to the most weak and vulnerable of all God's human creatures, the unborn. Abortion, he would say, is not a question of when life begins. It is a question of when love begins. "No insignificant person was ever born," he stated, "and no insignificant person ever dies." Casey was committed to upholding the working-class allegiance he associated with the presumed ideals of the Democratic Party, while that same Party was moving in the direction of abortion. He asserted that his Party's position on abortion "is inconsistent with our national character," and that it can "never prosper if it does not protect the powerless—before and after birth."

After attending Scranton Preparatory School, Casey turned down an offer to sign with the Philadelphia Phillies in 1949. Instead, he accepted a basketball scholarship to the College of Holy Cross where he was president of his senior class. After graduating with a Bachelor of Arts degree in 1953, he received a law degree from George Washington University three years later. He became Auditor General for the state of Pennsylvania and subsequently became its governor in 1986. Four years later, he was re-elected, defeating a pro-choice Republican by more than a million votes while carrying sixty-six of sixty-seven counties. It was the largest margin of victory in Pennsylvania gubernatorial history. During his tenure, Casey tried, though unsuccessfully, to establish universal health care for every Pennsylvania resident. He did, however, sign a bill providing health insurance for children of poor families who did not qualify for public medical assistance.

While governor, he did as much as he could to protect the unborn given the tight restrictions of *Roe v. Wade*. "In this country, the greatest country in the world," he stated, "every child deserves to be born." He could not accept the fact that America could "write off and leave behind an entire class of innocent, vulnerable and defenseless human beings." Planned Parenthood sued over his state's Abortion Control Act and the case was heard by the United States Supreme Court (*Planned Parenthood v. Casey*). The 1992 decision, which Casey called "a victory for the unborn child," affirmed the legality of a twenty-four-hour waiting period before obtaining an abortion, informed consent about health risks for women seeking abortion, parental consent for minors seeking abortion, and detailed record keeping on the abortion industry.

Casey was shunned by his own Democratic Party. At the 1992 Democratic convention in New York, he was kept from the podium by the Clinton-Gore ticket. In October of the same year, shouting pro-abortion protestors prevented him from speaking at Cooper Union in New York, where he intended to draw a connection between abortion and slavery on the very site where Abraham Lincoln once spoke. After being rejected as a speaker at the 1986 Chicago convention, Casey demanded that "those who believe in the right to life be accorded the right to speak." The ill treatment given to him by his own Party embarrasses and contradicts its own alleged commitment to fairness, democracy, and social justice issues.

Casey had aspirations for challenging Clinton in 1996 for the presidency of the United States. But his health was waning. Casey had bypass surgery in 1989. Four years later, suffering from a disease called "familial amyloidosis," he underwent a rare heart-liver transplant. It was also reported that he received radiation for prostate cancer. In the aftermath of his remarkable recovery, which extended his life and his trials by seven years, *The New York Times* dubbed him a "folk hero" for his courage and determination. His autobiography won a Christopher Award in 1997.

A challenge for the presidency was not to be his. On May 30, in the year 2000, Robert P. Casey passed from this world. Princeton University's Robert P. George lamented the loss, stating that "the pro-life movement has lost a champion, the Democratic Party its conscience, and American politics a model of principled statesmanship." He was survived by his wife, four sons, four daughters, and twenty grandchildren. One writer referred to the Caseys as the "G-rated version of the Kennedys."

It takes a man of humility to be a man of magnanimity. This is the central irony of the moral law. The man of pride can neither see straight nor love right. There is a moral line that flows from a stable in Bethlehem to a Doctor of the Catholic Church to a young Scranton coal miner and his numerous descendants that offers us the hope that humility will one day save the world.

PAINTING FOR LIFE

William Kurelek

I was about to take my aesthetics students to the Albright-Knox Art Gallery in Buffalo when a friend suggested that on my way there, I stop at the Niagara Falls Art Gallery and view the artistry of William Kurelek. And so I did, but what we found there was an unexpected treasure. We never did get to Buffalo.

The museum's centerpiece is 160 paintings illustrating as many verses from the passion of Christ according to St. Matthew. This ambitious project required six years of planning and execution, including a three-week sojourn in the Holy Land where Kurelek retraced the footsteps of Christ and three years in studying the Gospel. He commenced his work on New Year's Day 1960 and produced one painting per week until the series was completed. Slides were made from the paintings and shown by missionaries in various parts of the world.

The museum curators, Mykola and Ola Kolankiwsky, were more than gracious to us. A tri-lingual coffee-table edition of

the Passion series was in the works and Mykola invited me
to write an article for it. They were eager to introduce me to
Kurelek who was equally gracious, providing seven illustra-
tions for one book of mine and a cover for another. We met
on several occasions and exchanged letters. He would refer
to me as "The Professor," an accolade I felt was unwarranted,
given his extraordinary stature as an artist. I found him to be
attentive, humble, and the possessor of a sly sense of humor.

Patricia Morley begins her biography of Kurelek by stating that his life is "one of the strangest stories ever told." At
the same time, she acknowledges that "Kurelek is one of the
great painters which this country [Canada] has nurtured." It
is an odyssey that moves from self-doubt to despair, and then
from recovery to gratitude. It has strong affinities with Francis Thompson's celebrated poem "The Hound of Heaven,"
one that had been a personal favorite with Kurelek. For
him, no other poem expressed so completely his "personal
life lesson." He attached particular significance to the line,
"Nature, poor stepdame, cannot slake my drouth." Like
Thompson, Kurelek's story is one of fear and flight, grace
and redemption.

William Kurelek was born on a farm in 1927 to
Ukrainian-Canadian pioneers, near Whitford, Alberta. He
was the oldest of seven children. The first seven years if his
childhood were spent there, the next dozen in Stonewall,
Manitoba, just north of Winnipeg. Because of his hypersen-
sitive nature and his lack of athletic and mechanical abilities,
he was a persistent target of abuse from both his father as
well as his peers. In 1950, he decided to hitchhike to Mexico
to find a master painter. Caught in the cold night air of the

Arizona desert, he took refuge under a road bridge and went to sleep. In his autobiography, he records that the next thing he realized was that someone was with him. A man in a long white robe appeared, urging him to rise: "Get up, we must look after the sheep, or you will freeze to death." Kurelek interpreted this vision as an indication that he was not alone, that "Someone" was with him, and would remain with him throughout "the rest of my journey through this tragic, puzzling, yet wonderful world. There is Someone with me. And He has asked me to get up because there is work to be done."

His experience in the Arizona desert notwithstanding, Kurelek's fortunes turned from bad to worse. He went to England and checked into a psychiatric hospital where he received a series of excruciating electric convulsion treatments for chronic depression and acute eye pains. His condition, however, deteriorated. At his wits end, he slashed himself and crawled under his bed hoping to bleed to death. A hospital nurse entered his room at a propitious moment and saved his life.

A sympathetic occupational nurse by the name of Margaret Smith befriended him and introduced him to the Catholic faith. In February 1977, and after extensive preparation, the once staunch atheist entered the Catholic Church. Nurse Smith served as his godmother. At last he had a home that would not abandon him, nor would he ever abandon. He produced his Passion series out of gratitude to God for his healing. He attended Mass daily and became committed to two pressing issues: social justice and justice for the unborn child.

In his painting "It's Hard for Us to Realize," he juxtaposes the manicured plushness of the Rosedale Country Club with the poverty of India. He portrays overweight picnickers who are stuffing themselves with food while remaining oblivious to emaciated supplicant coolies. His film *Pacem in Terris,* inspired by Saint John XXIII's encyclical, is specifically directed to the critical need for social justice and the cooperation of nations in the world. Concerning his most graphic anti-abortion work, "Our My Lai, the Massacre of Highland Creek," he compares aborted babies with the slaughter of innocent and helpless citizens in Vietnam. He depicts buckets filled with the aborted unborn and their blood flowing across a snowy landscape and over the painting's frame.

On the positive side of things, he donated money he earned from his paintings to pro-life organizations such as Birthright and Right to Life. A Mississauga couple paid $5,000 for one of his works which went directly to Toronto Right to Life. He and his wife had four children, two of whom were adopted. They also have foster children in difference parts of the globe. The money he earned for each "cow" he painted paid for an actual cow for the poor in Brazil. At first, he kept track of how many cows he provided by naming them after family members. But he soon ran out of names.

Kurelek produced sixteen books illustrating his paintings from "O Toronto" to "Prairie Boy's Summer." For his various achievements, he was made a member of the Order of Canada and the Royal Canadian Academy of Arts. He is honored by a number of national and international awards. He painted for life and perhaps exhausted himself in the process. Sadly, he died of cancer in 1977 at fifty years of age.

The Apostle of Life

Paul Marx

Saint Thomas Aquinas was most particular when he offered singular praise for his esteemed predecessors: Aristotle was "*the* Philosopher," Moses Maimonides was "*the* Rabbi," and St. Paul was "*the* Apostle." We have reason to believe that Pope Saint John Paul II was just as particular when he called his esteemed friend, Fr. Paul Marx, OSB, "The Apostle of Life." The appellation is well deserved and was used as a title for Fr. Marx's 1991 book that is an account of his work for Human Life International. This "apostle," at that time, had carried the pro-life message personally to more than 90 countries and shipped pro-life material to 111. "Dear Father Marx," wrote James D. Sangu, Bishop of Mbeya, Tanzania, "You are indeed the Apostle of Human Life Protection."

The Apostle of Life [42] is also an urgent plea to his readers to join him "and all the other Apostles of Life to work among our thirty-eight international branches as we do what the

---

[42]   Paul Marx, *The Apostle of Life* (Gaithersburg, Md: Human Life International, 1991).

Holy Father calls the most important work on earth." In contrast with St. Paul, who was an apostle, traveler, and a writer, Fr. Marx was an apostle, traveler, and a fighter, as was made evident in another book of his which he called *Fighting for Life.*[43]

In order to understand the genesis of Fr. Marx's missionary zeal for life and his clear recognition that the abortion establishment was imperilling civilization, we turn the clock back to a conference that took place at the International Hotel in Los Angeles, January 22–24, 1971. The theme of the conference was "Therapeutic Abortion: a Symposium on Implementation." Since Fr. Marx was a professor of sociology, he attended the conference under that title. He brought with him a tape recorder. What he discovered, and recorded, became grist for his best-selling book *The Death Peddlers: War on the Unborn.*[44]

At that time, abortion was legal only in seventeen states. Nonetheless, the rate of abortion was increasing rapidly, and the climate of the culture was moving inexorably toward a permissive abortion law on a national level. The keynote speaker was Dr. Leon Israel, professor of obstetrics and gynecology at the University of Pennsylvania school of Medicine. He discussed "The Liberation of Women from Unwanted Pregnancy" and set the tone for the conference. Anticipating the infamous *Roe v. Wade* decision exactly two years later, in 1973, he declared, "Early interruption of pregnancy, poorly

---

43   Paul Marx and Gerald E. Murray, T*he Flying Monk: Still Fighting for Life* (Gaithersburg: Human Life International, 1990).

44   Paul Marx, *The Death Peddlers: War on the Unborn* (Collegeville, Minn: Saint John's University Press, 1971).

called 'abortion,' is a female right." Dr. J. G. Moore, professor and chairman of obstetrics and gynecology of the School of Medicine at UCLA offered three reasons why there must be abortion: to control population, to ensure that the family can properly educate the children they want, and because it is a mother's right. Dr. Robert E. Hall, associate professor of obstetrics and gynecology at Columbia University's College of Physicians and Surgeons, foresaw a golden age of easy abortion and sexual freedom without compulsory motherhood, an age inaugurated by a multiform abortion law."

"In this crazy world of the abortion symposium," wrote Fr. Marx, "a man may lose touch with the realities of life and love, honor and duty, human dignity and divine transcendence." At the symposium, abortion is called "back-up contraception," the unborn child is "a product of conception, a contraceptive failure, and a 'mistake.'" A lawyer suggests that the unborn need an advocate for their death, a clergyman defends the fetal right not to be born, and a theologian calls it blind religiosity to speak of unborn babies. A passage from G. K. Chesterton's *Ballad of the White Horse* comes to mind: "I tell you naught for your comfort, yea naught for your desire, save that the sky grows darker yet, and the sea rises higher." It was time to act, and Fr. Paul Marx certainly answered the bell.

As Fr. Marx affirmed in his autobiography, *Faithful for Life*, published in 2008, that this kind of experience of the pro-abortionists made him realize without a doubt that from that point on "the developing culture of death would preoccupy me for the rest of my life and would take me to many countries of the world."[45] All in all, he traveled to ninety-one countries spreading the pro-life message. His life was not easy, but he was blessed. He was arrested three times. Planned Parenthood, which sued him, dubbed him as "public enemy number one." What was more difficult for him to accept was the vilification he received from members of his own order. On the other hand, he survived three nearly-fatal car crashes, was forcibly removed from several abortuaries, almost died from the high altitude while in the Bolivian mountains, and should have been on the fatal Pan Am Flight 103 that was blown up over Lockerbie, Scotland in 1988. God is also an apostle of life.

Personally, I remain indebted to Fr. Marx. He was instrumental in the publication of my first book—*Abortion in Perspective: The Rose Palace or the Fiery Dragon*. He invited me to speak at several of his conferences. We kept in touch. In the last letter I received from him, he praised my book, *New Perspectives in Contraception*, as the best book on the subject he had ever read. And I am most grateful to serve as a "Senior Fellow" for Human Life International in the capacity of a writer.

Paul Marx was born on a dairy farm in the town of St. Michael, Minnesota, the fifteenth of seventeen children. That small community of 2,500 people has produced more than one hundred priests and nuns. When Fr. Marx, OSB, passed away on March 20, 2010, his obituary in the *Daily Catholic* read as follows: "Father Paul resided at the Abbey

---

45   Paul Marx, *Faithful for Life* (Front Royal, Va: Human Life International, 1997).

in Collegeville, but also continued to write when he could and prayed constantly for life in all its stages. Throughout his forty-seven years of service for the cause, Father Marx not only provided encouragement to pro-life advocates the world over, but, in God's Great Book, gave life to many of His innocent ones who would not have had a chance to enter the world without the efforts of this 'Apostle of Life.'"

AN APOSTLE OF MANY GIFTS

Archbishop Fulton Sheen

No historical account of Catholicism in twentieth-century America would be complete without mention of Archbishop Fulton J. Sheen, whose gifts were as rich as they were varied. He was born on May 8, 1895 in the small town of El Paso, Illinois and died eighty-four years later, on December 9 in the metropolis of New York City, the day after the Feast of the Immaculate Conception. He is buried in the crypt at St. Patrick's Cathedral. The cause for his canonization was officially opened in 2002 in the Diocese of Peoria, Illinois. Pope Benedict XVI, in recognition of Archbishop Sheen's heroic virtue and life of sanctity, bestowed upon him, in 2012, the title "Venerable."

Archbishop Sheen seemed to embody, more than any other figure of his time, all that was good about Catholicism in America. He made it easy for Catholics to be proud of their faith and others to envy it. The Jesuit magazine *America* called him "the greatest evangelist in the history of the Catholic Church in the United States." One journalist remarked, "No

Catholic bishop has burst on the world with such power as Sheen wields since long before the Protestant Reformation."

He won an Emmy Award for "Most Outstanding Television Personality" in 1952, beating out show biz giants such as Lucille Ball, Arthur Godfrey, and Edward R. Murrow. Upon receiving the prize, he said, "I wish to thank my four writers: Matthew, Mark, Luke and John." Between 1952 and 1956, according to a Gallup Poll, he was one of America's ten most admired men. From 1952 to 1957 there were 127 episodes of his *Life Is Worth Living* television program. A total of 113 television stations and 300 radio stations carried the program in 1956 to an estimated 30 million viewers and listeners. "*Life Is Worth Living,*" as one authoritative book on television attested, "was probably the most viewed religion series in TV history."

Sheen authored sixty-six books and sixty-two booklets. He maintained a staggering work pace of nineteen-hour days, seven days a week. He was the head of the Propagation of the Faith and involved in innumerable fund-raising programs for the Mission and for the poor. He seemed to incorporate all that was good about Catholicism within the frame of a single person.

Archbishop Sheen's life, though based on prayer and meditation, was lived, to a large extent, in the spotlight. He hobnobbed with celebrities, notable ecclesiastics, and dignitaries (though never ignoring the ordinary man on the street). He was instrumental in the conversions of Fritz Kreisler, Loretta Young, Clare Booth Luce, Virginia Mayo, Heywood Broun, and Louis Budenz, then managing editor the *Daily Worker,* the Communist Party newspaper in America. Much of what

Sheen has offered the world applies even to our time, and he said it with eloquent simplicity.

As a good philosopher, he understood that truth is eternal. Therefore, he was aggrieved that it could facilely be demoted and replaced by novelty, fashion, or whatever happens to be *au courant*. An encounter with Samuel Alexander while Sheen was a graduate student at the University of Louvain offers a case in point. Professor Alexander's book *Space, Time, and Deity* had created somewhat of a sensation. The author had proposed a novel view of God as the deification of time and space. Sheen, who, at that time, was working on his thesis, *God and Intelligence in the Modern World*, asked him if he would be interested in reading the philosophy of Thomas Aquinas. Alexander's response was perfectly in synchrony with the climate of his time: "No, I would not be interested because you become known in this world not through Truth, but through novelty, and my doctrine is novel." It was clear enough to Sheen that his adversary was more interested in what is novel than what is enduring.

Samuel Alexander's views were novel in 1922. He had his moment of fame. But his contribution has failed the test of time. He is no longer novel, and no longer in the public consciousness. The thought of Aquinas and Sheen continue to be both important and relevant. Truth is eternal; novelty is ephemeral. The Press is for today, but not for tomorrow. When C. S. Lewis remarked, "All that is not eternal is eternally out of date," he did not have in mind that something novel could be up-to-date for even a brief moment. To be novel is to be eternally out of date because novelty does not belong to the continuing stream of time. It is a deviation, a diversion, a distraction.

Archbishop Sheen passed away six years after *Roe v. Wade*. What he had to say about the sanctity of life as an enduring truth is as timely today as it always has been. Two years and three days after the ill-fated Supreme Court decision, he made the following comment: "In ancient Rome, there was a *potestas patria* or the right of the father to dispose of a child. In our modern day, there is the *potesta matria* or the right of the mother to dispose of a child. In between pagan Rome and today there was, and still is, a group of God-loving people who will protect those who are incapable of independent existence because they sense in their own frailty the mercy of God and, therefore, resolve to extend it to others." In this instance, truth was demoted and replaced by convenience.

Sheen also reminded people how abortion violates the Golden Rule. If defects are a basis for the destruction of life, he reasoned, then we should remember that for the first three centuries, Christians were regarded as "defective" and so were Jews in the mind of Hitler, and property owners in the view of Communists. Furthermore, a child that is born might one day claim the right to euthanize his mother if she has the "defect" of senility or simply of old age.

Archbishop Sheen closes his autobiography, *Treasure in Clay*, by acknowledging God's goodness on his behalf, manifested by the gifts of Christian parents, a fine education, and sundry other gifts.[46] But then he writes: "The greatest gift of all may be His summons to the Cross, where I found His continuing self-disclosure." In death, as Scripture tells us, there is life.

---

[46]   Fulton J. Sheen, *Treasure in Clay: The Autobiography of Fulton J. Sheen*, (Garden City, NY: Doubleday, Inc., 1980).

Clare Boothe Luce

The name Clare Boothe Luce is one that should not remain absent from the minds of contemporary Catholics. She may not have been a saint but was vitally concerned about how much a saint can do to restore a backward culture. She understood only too well that in times of crisis we need saints. In 1952 she edited a classic entitled *Saints for Now*.[47] It was a compilation of twenty essays written by twenty distinguished authors (mostly Catholic) about their favorite saints and how much these servants of God meant to the times in which they lived. In her introduction, Mrs. Luce made the following comment:

> We live in an intellectual climate of ambiguity, of multiple and conflicting "truths," of exclusive and warring "freedoms." In a world where truth is relative, where one man's "truth" is another man's "lie," and his definition of "freedom" is his neighbor's definition of

---

[47]   Clare Boothe Luce, *Saints for Now* (New York: Sheed & Ward, 1952).

"slavery," plainly the burden of carrying the argument
. . . must fall on an appeal not to the mind, but to
the emotions. Advertising, propaganda—the sophisticated tools of irrationalism—supersede fact, persuasion and logic, the tools of reason.

Pulitzer Prize winner Phyllis McGinley reiterated the
point in *Saint-Watching* when she stated, "Ours is an age of
violence and disbelief. But in spite of that, or because of it,
the earth's interest in virtuous accomplishment is stronger
now than it has been at any time since the Age of Reason
began ousting religion from its seat of authority."[48]

The "now" that Luce described better than six decades ago
and McGinley lamented seventeen years later seems an apt
description of the "now" of the present. *Plus ça change, plus
c'est la même chose* ("The more things change, the more they
stay the same"). Three questions leap to mind: Are cultures
always confused and divided? Is it futile to insist on reason
and logic? Who are the saints of today that will rescue culture from ruin? McGinley believes "they may well be rising
among us now, preparing to lead us out of the onrushing
night which so threateningly descends." The "now" should
not be dissolved by the following moment in time but should
be prevented from passing into oblivion by connecting it
with what is timeless. This is the office of the saint.

Clare Luce was led into the Church by Fulton Sheen and
was often referred to as America's most famous Catholic
convert. Her talents were various and prodigious. She was a

---

[48]   Phyllis McGinley, *Saint-Watching* (New York: Viking Press,
1969).

novelist, a playwright, editor, essayist, philanthropist, member of Congress, diplomat, and Ambassador to both Italy and Brazil. The opening night of her play, *Margin for Error*, which is an all-out attack on the Nazi's racist philosophy, was attended by Albert Einstein and Thomas Mann. Several of her plays were adapted to the screen. In 1983 President Reagan awarded her the Presidential Medal of Freedom. She was the first member of Congress to receive this award.

She was a critic of her times (and, prophetically, of the current times as well). Yet she understood how difficult it may be to shed one's prejudices and think objectively and rationally. On one occasion, she confronted her house guest, the renowned philosopher Mortimer Adler, who, staring blankly at his feet, seemed bored. When she asked him if there was something he would like to do, noting her puzzlement, he explained: "I'm thinking. And that's the hardest thing in the world, because, you see, when you really want to think a question through, you've got to begin by laying all your prejudices on the table. And that's the toughest thing for anyone to do, even for a philosopher."

Mrs. Luce deplored the fact that the defenders of abortion had virtually nothing to say in defense of their position. She thought that the most dismaying thing about the abortion controversy might be that "many intelligent people go intellectually to pieces when confronted with the core question: Is an unborn child a human being?" (*The Human Life Review*, Winter, 1977). She reminded the world that "no Supreme Court ruling is considered infallible." It was an important message she has left to posterity. As she went on to explain, "Historically the Court has been prone to reflect the political mood (and emotional prejudices) of the public, and as the mood changed or new facts emerged, the Court has often reversed itself . . . as in the case of the Dred Scott decision, the Court's decision has been reversed by amendment to the Constitution when it ceased to reflect a public consensus."

She wrote "A Letter to the Women's Lobby" in which she opposed the feminist campaign against pro-life political candidates. Her statement, printed in italics for emphasis, could not have been more forceful or more definitive: "*There is no logical process of thought by which the unnatural act of induced abortion and the destruction of the unborn child in the womb can be deemed to be a natural right of all women*" (*The Human Life Review*, Spring, 1978). Clare Boothe Luce was a Woman among women.

Clare Boothe Luce once remarked, "Courage is the ladder on which all the other virtues mount." There can be no sanctity without courage, including the courage to stand against contemporary prejudices and hold firm to what is true. Moreover, there can be no virtue without courage, and a culture without virtue is indeed destitute. And what is sanctity? It is, as Phyllis McGinley avers, and Mrs. Luce would most certainly endorse, "the world's strangest and highest form of genius." Culture should welcome such geniuses as the music world embraces Bach, Beethoven, and Brahms. But first, culture must lay aside its own prejudices and open itself to truths that transcend time.

Clare Boothe Luce passed away on October 9, 1987 at the age of eighty-four. She is buried at Mepkin Abbey, South Carolina, a plantation that she and her husband, Henry

Luce, had given to a community of Trappist monks. May her legacy and their prayers be a source of healing for our battered times.

Eugenio Zolli

In the summer of 1944, two events helped to establish Pope Pius XII's reputation as a rescuer of Jews. When the Allies liberated Rome, thousands of Jewish people emerged from their hiding places and told the world of the debt they owed to the Vatican for saving their lives. "It is gradually being revealed," the *Jewish News* in Detroit reported (July 7, 1944), "that Jews have been sheltered within the walls of the Vatican during the German occupation of Rome." A July 14 editorial in the *Congress Weekly*, the official journal of the American Jewish Congress, added that the Vatican even provided Jewish refugees with kosher food.

The second event was more personal. On July 14 of that same year, *American Hebrew* in New York published an interview with Chief Rabbi Israel Zolli of Rome. "The Vatican has always helped the Jews," he stated, "and the Jews are very grateful for the charitable work of the Vatican, all done without distinction of race." A *New York Times* piece reported Rabbi Zolli stating that "the Pope and the Vatican were indefatigable in working to save Jews and many hundreds were sheltered in monasteries and convents in Rome and in Vatican City" (June 17, 1944).

After the war, on February 13, 1945, Zolli converted to Catholicism. Out of his profound respect for Pius XII (Eugenio Pacelli), he took "Eugenio" as his baptismal name. Zolli's conversion was widely attributed to his gratitude for what Pius XII did for the Jews. He strenuously denied this. In his 1954 memoirs, *Before the Dawn* (later published as *Why I Became a Catholic*), he claimed to have witnessed a vision of Christ, who called him to the Faith. Yet his conversion was not simply the result of a supernatural occurrence. "I was a Catholic at heart before the war broke out: and I promised God in 1943 that I should become a Christian if I survived the war. No one in the world ever tried to convert me. My conversion was a slow evolution, altogether internal." Zolli's wife and daughter also entered the Church.

Why was the pope's involvement in helping the Jews in dispute? It began with the fictitious play by Rolf Hochhuth entitled *The Deputy*. The play and its negative impact on Pius XII was a well-crafted plan called "Seat Twelve" hatched and implemented by the KGB to defame the Catholic Church. The play accused Pius XII of being anti-Semitic and a collaborator of Adolf Hitler. It is regarded as one of the most effective examples of character assassinations in modern history. Sir Martin Gilbert, a world-renowned historian of WWII condemned it as a "well-crafted fiction not at all based on historical evidence."

Nonetheless the impact of the play has been difficult to overcome. The so-called "silence of Pius XII" was used by many people who should have known better. When the US Conference of Catholic Bishops, for example, criticized former US Surgeon General Dr. Joycelyn Elders for her pro-abortion views, she responded by alleging the Church's indifference toward the Holocaust. Hochhuth's demonic portrayal of the pope had become accepted in certain circles as conventional wisdom. On the other hand, for people who were more interested in facts than fiction, Pinchas Lapide, Israeli Ambassador and historian, states that Pius XII deserves a memorial forest in the Judean Hills with 860,000 trees, corresponding to the number of Jewish lives that were saved through papal efforts. Lapide reports his finding in *The Last Three Popes and the Jews* (*The New York Times*, April 24, 1966, page 13). According to Lapide, "The Catholic Church saved more Jewish lives during the war than all other churches, religious institutions and rescue organizations put together."

Expressions of gratitude from Jewish communities for the pope's work in saving the lives of so many Jews are innumerable. Let one example suffice. Preaching at the Temple Israel in New York, Rev. Dr. William F. Rosenblum praised both the pope as well as Catholics the world over, stating that Pope Pius XII, "during the Hitler holocaust . . . made it possible for thousands of Jewish victims of Nazism and Fascism to be hidden away in the monasteries and convents of the various Catholic orders and for Jewish children to be taken into their orphanages" (*The New York Times*, October 12, 1958). He lauded the pope as "a great religious leader whose work for brotherliness and peace in a time of crisis in our history should remain as an example for all religious leaders to emulate."

In the preface of his autobiography, Zolli begins by stating, "The figure of the crucified Christ over the altar symbolizes the greatest sorrow the world knows. Truth is crucified; the highest Wisdom, the Wisdom of God, is crucified." Truth continues to be crucified, the truth of the unborn child, of abortion and its effects on women, the family, and society. Zolli tells us that he "was deeply impressed by the words of Jesus: 'I am the light'; 'I am the way, the Truth, the Life.'" When Zolli was asked why he did not become a Protestant. "Because," he replied, "protesting is not attesting." Attesting to the truth, to Christ, to life is what is essential. He affirmed that God's very nature forbids his giving to the world, at any time, more than one religion. He did not view his conversion as precisely that: "The Synagogue pointed to Christianity: Christianity presupposes the Synagogue. So you see, one cannot exist without the other. What I converted to was the living Christianity."

War is an assault on life and on the dignity of the human being. But it is also an assault on Truth. When Truth is crucified, war becomes inevitable. "Where Christ is, there is Life," Zolli wrote in his memoir (p. 132). The world, if it is to avoid future wars, needs to undergo a conversion. Zolli's conversion was truly Christ-centered, although it paid homage to Pius XII. As he stated in his autobiography, "I did not hesitate to give a negative answer to the question whether I was converted in gratitude to Pius XII for his numberless acts of charity. Nevertheless, I do feel the duty of rendering homage and of affirming that the charity of the Gospel was the light that's showed the way to my old and weary heart. It is the charity that so often shines in the history of the Church and which radiated fully in the actions of the reigning Pontiff" (p. 189).

Charles Rice

I received a telephone call one day from a university col-league asking for my help. She had invited Professor Charles E. Rice, an expert on natural law, to speak and because of that was receiving death threats. I could not be of much help since I was about to leave the country on a teaching assignment. She had notified the police and was assured that they would provide adequate security. Professor Rice delivered his lecture with police protection in the room. The threats were taken seriously, however, and other presen-tations that Professor Rice was scheduled to make while he was in the area were cancelled.

Ironically, Professor Rice was not planning on talking about the natural law. Such is the temper of the times! The natural law provides an objective ground for constructing the argument that certain sexual acts, such as sodomy, are unnatural. It is a far more reasonable ground from which to construct moral argumentation than intimidating people by making threats of violence. It is a sad commentary on our times that reason is often suppressed so that force can set the agenda.

Who is Charles E. Rice? He was a specialist in constitutional law and jurisprudence, edited *The American Journal of Jurisprudence*, was a colorful and popular teacher, a Marine, a boxing coach, author of thirteen books, a staunch pro-life supporter, father of ten children and an adopted son born in South Vietnam, and grandfather of forty-one grandchildren. He served as a consultant to the US Commission on Civil Rights and to various congressional committees on constitutional issues and was a sought-after speaker. Rev. Wilson Miscamble, CSC, a friend and colleague of Professor Rice, said of him what many people who knew him could also have said: "His contribution as a teacher and scholar in the Law School influenced at least two generations of students to become lawyers who saw their work as a vocation and not just a career. His profound commitment to the pro-life cause and to the truths of natural law, which were so evident in his writings, and in his speaking and television appearances, gave him an influence far beyond the Notre Dame campus."

Charlie Rice was born in Manhattan on August 7, 1931. He received a bachelor's degree from the College of the Holy Cross in Worcester, MA, his law degree from Boston College Law School, and his master's and doctoral degree in law from New York University. He met his wife, Mary, at the Boston College Law School, practiced law in New York City, and taught at the New York University Law School and at Fordham Law School before joining the faculty at Notre Dame in 1969.

When I spoke at the Notre Dame Law School, Professor

Rice gave me *carte blanche* access to the law library. My research proved beneficial, not only by placing an article in a law review but providing my benefactor for more ammunition that he later used in his talks. He could not have been more encouraging and considerate. There are few, if any, people I have ever met that were easier to befriend than Charlie Rice.

His writing is straightforward, easy to read, and to the point. He is as keenly aware of moral philosophy as he is about the waywardness of the modern era. In his book *Beyond Abortion: The Theory and Practice of the Secular State* (1979), he illustrates in a striking way how things have changed for the worse.[49] He cites an auction held in Louisiana where a lady won her bid of $30 for an abortion at the Delta Women's Clinic. The auction was a fund-raising event sponsored by the American Civil Liberties Union. Rice makes the comment that that event "calls to mind the slave auctions so rhetorically opposed by the ACLU in other situations." In another sense, and on the subject of the family, has American society changed all that much since the time of pagan Rome? "We have finally caught up with the pagan Romans," he states, "who endowed the father, the paterfamilias, with the right to kill the child at his discretion. We give that right to the mother. But it is all the same to the victim." The situation is dire, but never too dire for prayer.

How does one understand the binding power of the opening words of the Declaration of Independence: "that all men are created equal, that they are endowed by their Creator with certain inalienable Rights, that among these

---

[49]   Charles E. Rice, *Beyond Abortion: The Theory and Practice of the Secular State* (Chicago: Franciscan Herald Press, 1979).

are Life, Liberty and the pursuit of Happiness?" For many, it is the consent of the people. But, as Rice argues, some laws are unjust no matter what the majority says. Drawing on the thought of Saint Thomas Aquinas, Professor Rice argues that human law must be in conformity with natural law. Therefore, there must be something more than the consent of the people that gives the Declaration of Independence is binding power, its ultimate legitimacy. The right to Life, therefore, is not based on consent. Rather, consent must be based on something higher; namely, the natural law that is ordained by God.

Ever the realist, he recognized the growing persecution of the Catholic Church in the United States. He anticipated an "inevitable" clash between the secular state and the Catholic Church on issues of family, the right to life, economic justice, and issues related to same-sex marriage. He saw the institution of federal mandates requiring Catholic employers to provide insurance coverage for contraception and sterilization as a salient example of "this accelerating persecution of the Church and of believing Catholics."

Charlie Rice died on February 25, 2015 at the age of eighty-three at the University of Chicago Medical Center surrounded by his loving family. He was a fighting Irishman for the Lord without ever disregarding the rules, and a teacher for his legion of listeners without ever compromising his integrity. His legacy will not be ignored and will serve to help restore the fundamental and irreplaceable role of the natural law in establishing the true basis for human rights, while assisting in the effort to overcome the grave moral division that currently divides America.

Mary Ann Glendon

Mary Ann Glendon was born on October 7, 1938, in Dalton, Massachusetts, a small town nestled in the Berkshire Hills. Her father was an Irish Catholic, her mother a Yankee Congregationalist. She learned a great deal from her mother's religion about social organization and from her father, how Catholicism "enlarged the spirit, gave wings to the imagination, and lent meaning to suffering." Catholic ceremonies, as she wrote, "spoke to me of a history before Plymouth Rock, and its liturgy linked me to every living Catholic on earth."

This openness to the lessons of history and the dignity of all human beings set the tone for her subsequent career in comparative law and as an advocate of universal rights. Catholicism was her bulwark. "Amid the tug-and-pull of special interests and power politics," she stated, "the Church has stood clearly, and often alone, for *all* the freedoms that flow from the image and likeness of God." Given her broad outlook, it was reasonable, therefore, that she would cultivate a strong affection for Plato who was able to synthesize philosophy, law, and the good of society. The University of Chicago, where such stalwarts such as Mortimer Adler, Richard Weaver, and Leo Strauss were teaching, while Catholic luminaries such as Jacques Maritain and Martin D'Arcy were frequent lecturers, attracted her.

She received her Bachelor of Arts, *Juris Doctor*, and Master of Comparative Law from the University of Chicago, practiced law in Chicago from 1963–68, taught at the Boston College Law School and commenced her long tenure at Harvard Law School in 1987. In 1995, Pope John Paul II appointed her head of the Vatican delegation to the United Nations Conference in Beijing and, in 2004, named her president of the Pontifical Academy of Social Science. In 2007 the US Senate confirmed her as ambassador to the Holy See. From 2001–2004, she served on President George W. Bush's Council on Bioethics.

The study of law sharpens the mind and broadens one's scope. These words, it appears, have served as a guiding principle throughout Mary Ann Glendon's distinguished career. The law sharpens the mind by making distinctions such as those between guilty and not-guilty, good and bad, true and false, and relevant and irrelevant. At the same time, it broadens one's scope to include the many factors that are pertinent to a particular case. The law, for example, should avoid oversimplification and exclusion.

Dr. Glendon has been a stern critic of *Roe v. Wade*, to a large extent because of its narrow focus and, consequently, what it ignores. In her 1987 award-winning book, *Abortion and Divorce in Western Law*, she employs Plato's method of comparative law in examining the laws on those two subjects in twenty countries.[50] Her conclusion is that the abortion laws in the United States reflect an attitude that is most impoverished. This is because *Roe v. Wade* is narrowly based on the view of the woman as an autonomous person, an individual who has a constitutional right to abort. In that landmark 1973 decision, Justice Blackmun was careful not to describe the fetus as either alive or as a person. To take one contrasting example, Helmut Kohl, who served as Chancellor of Germany from 1982–1998, attested that his government's policy concerning abortion "is to increase maternity benefits and child allowances to help people with raising children." *Roe v. Wade*, given its absolute emphasis on the right of the mother, precludes such discussion.

Law is not simply a command backed up by a system of enforcement. As Mary Ann Glendon is at pains to point out, law tells a story. It tells a story about who we are, our origins, our future prospects, and what we value as citizens. The abortion laws in America tell a highly truncated story: that abortion is a matter of individual, private choice and the human fetus is not a person. Law also carries an exalted significance. The protagonist of Plato's *Laws* is a traveler from his native city, an old man who does not have a name. Plato refers to him as the Athenian Stranger. The Stranger asks: "Is it a god or some human being who is given credit for laying down your laws?" Although it is left to human beings

---

50   Mary Ann Glendon, *Abortion and Divorce in Western Law* (Cambridge, Mass: Harvard University Press, 1989).

to legislate, they should not be unaware of the transcendent implications that laws can represent.

In another of Glendon's award-winning books, *Rights Talk*, she criticizes the one-sidedness of the radical individualism that is part of the American tradition.[51] She offers examples of how rights without corresponding duties create very disturbing situations. In one case, operators of a boat-rental service sat on the shore of a lake and watched an inebriated customer lose his grip on his overturned canoe and drown. A Massachusetts Supreme Judicial Court voted unanimously that the defendants were under no legal obligation to heed the drowning man's screams. In a similar case, one judge stated that a person has no obligation to come to the rescue of an endangered child: "I am not liable in damages to the child for his injuries . . . because the child and I are strangers, and I am under no legal duty to protect him."

Glendon sees this one-sidedness—rights without corresponding duties—as inimical to community. A true community is a fellowship of persons, not an aggregate of individuals or a collectivity of bystanders. Just as Glendon offers a voice for the unborn, she also offers a helping hand to those who are distressed.

Consistent with her pro-life, communitarian views, Dr. Glendon created a stir in 2009 when she declined acceptance of Notre Dame University's *Laetare Medal*. In a letter to President Jenkins, CSC, which she made public, she reminded the president that his invitation to pro-abortion

---

[51]   Mary Ann Glendon, *Rights Talk: The Impoverishment of Political Discourse* (New York: Free Press, 1991).

Barack Obama to give the Commencement Address was in disregard "of the U. S. bishops' express request of 2004 that Catholic institutions 'should not honor those who act in defiance of our fundamental moral principles' and that such persons 'should not be given awards, honors or platforms which would suggest support for their actions.'"

Dr. Glendon received an award more in keeping with her convictions from the National Right to Life Committee at its Pro-Life Awards Dinner in 2014. Academic excellence and moral integrity make a beautiful marriage.

PART VII

Apostles From the World At Large

George Gilder

George Gilder, together with his wife and four children, have adopted the charming town of Tyringham—a virtual art colony nestled in the Berkshire Hills of western Massachusetts—as their home. His fame and influence have not interfered with his domestic stability. Nor have the PC police, though not without making a concerted effort, succeeded in stifling his creativity. He offers hope for all those who may be intimidated by the power of political correctness to stick to their guns and find their own way of achieving prosperity.

Gilder became a target for the politically correct brigade with his book *Sexual Suicide.*[52] It earned him the wrath of the National Organization for Women and the label "Male Chauvinist Pig of the Year." He won the designation, according to *Time* magazine, with a "one-punch knockout

---

52   George F. Gilder, *Sexual Suicide* (New York: Bantam Books, 1975).

of Norman Mailer." He was, for secular feminists, public enemy number one.

What was so incendiary about *Sexual Suicide*? Gilder dared to affirm the complementarity of the sexes, the importance of love and marriage, and a critique of the excesses of secular feminism. He went so far as to praise the Catholic Church for insisting on the unity between sexual intimacy and procreation. In retrospect, this work, published in 1973, appears prophetic and would be even more politically incorrect today than when it first appeared. The ensuing paragraph gets to the heart of the matter: "Gay liberation, pornographic glut, and one-night trysts are all indices of sexual frustration; all usually disclose a failure to achieve profound and loving sexuality. When a society deliberately affirms these failures—contemplates legislation of homosexual marriage, celebrates the women who denounce the family, and indulges pornography as a manifestation of sexual health and a release from repression—the culture is promoting a form of erotic suicide."

The reaction to *Sexual Suicide* was not merely verbal. Invitations to speak at universities were withdrawn, feminists shouted him down when he tried to speak, for example, on the Dick Cavett Show, other outraged feminists threatened to strike at several publishing houses if Gilder were taken on as an author. Gilder realized that the marketplace of free ideas was not open to anyone who questioned the assumptions of radical feminism. Most bookstores would not order or stock *Sexual Suicide*. Publishers boycotted his next work, *Men and Marriage* (1992), though Pelican, a small press in Louisiana, was willing to take a chance on it. In that work,

Gilder makes it clear that he has no animus against women.[53] "The crucial problem of civilization," he writes, "is the subordination of male sexual impulses and biology to the long-term horizons of female sexuality." Because of the "sexual superiority of women," he goes on to say, "women transform male lust into love . . . conceive the future that men tend to flee. . . . The womb and breasts bear a message of immortality."

Undaunted, Gilder wrote *Wealth and Poverty*, which became a best-seller.[54] It became the "Bible" of President Reagan's administration's supply-siders. Gilder became the one living author whom Reagan quoted most often in his speeches. *Wealth and Poverty* is a defense and celebration of capitalism. The author strongly disagrees with those who regard greed as the driving force of the economy. For Gilder, truly greedy people want to be compensated far beyond what is just. "Greed," he states, "leads as by an invisible hand to socialism." By contrast, "Capitalism begins with giving. Not from greed, avarice, or even self-love can one expect the rewards of commerce, but from a spirit closely akin to altruism, a regard for the needs of other, a benevolent, outgoing, and courageous temper of mind."

Gilder praises papal encyclicals for their denunciation of materialism: "Thus the Pope [John Paul II] is completely consonant with capitalism when he denounces materialism. Materialism is the perennial enemy—and temptation—of

---

53   George F. Gilder, *Men and Marriage* (Gretna, La: Pelican Pub. Co., 1992).
54   George F. Gilder, *Wealth and Poverty* (New York: Basic Books, 1980).

capitalism." Capitalism, he argues, needs the spiritual and religious foundations provided by churches and schools that believe in the "the paramount natural laws of giving and faith." He has little regard for secular culture, which he finds "corrupt, degraded, and depraved." Nor is he particularly enamored with what passes for higher education, especially in the humanities. At a great many of the elite universities, he contends, worthless courses in nihilism, relativism, feminism, and Marxism are taught.

Gilder's more recent books deal with technology, its innovations, and its potentialities for a better world. Among his special interests are quantum mechanics, the new microcosm world, transistors, silicon chips, and the teleputer. He is a co-founder of the Discovery Institute whose home base is in Seattle, WA. The institute affirms the representative democracy as expounded by the Founding Fathers and the belief in God-given reason, the permanency of human nature, and the social requirement to balance liberty with responsibility.

Gilder has prospered for several reasons that mainly relate to his character. We may list six: 1) do not make concessions to your enemies; 2) stick to your guns; 3) understand the primacy of spirit; 4) become knowledgeable of many things; 5) get ahead of the game; 6) be grounded in a strong family. If there are to be great accomplishments in the future, they will be made by people who did not allow themselves to be checked at the door by political correctness. Gilder's example should serve as model for all.

In discussing the complementarity between science and religion, he finds special meaning that the quantum vision offers in the form of a "cross of light." "Combining a particle and a wave," he writes, "it [the light] joins the definite to the infinite, a point of mass to an eternal radiance." "What else would a Christian expect to find at the foundations of the world?" he asks. "In this light, we can comprehend the paradox of the brain and the mind, the temporal and the divine, flesh and the word, freedom and fatality. By this light, we can even find the truth." The intellectual life is a journey to ends that are yet to be discovered, let alone understood. Political correctness is an abject surrender to the *status quo*.

Hellen Hull Hitchcock

Helen Hull Hitchcock passed away after a brief illness on October 20, 2014 at age seventy-five. Accolades poured in from around the globe in honor of this extraordinary woman. Mary Shivanandan, a retired faculty member at the Pontifical John Paul II Institute for studies on Marriage and the Family and a long-time friend of Helen, provided a concise and accurate summation of Mrs. Hitchcock's life and contribution to the Church: "In the midst of an increasingly secular culture and a strident feminism, Helen embodied the true 'woman's genius' of John Paul II by bringing to bear her feminine gifts to the pressing problems of our day without compromising her role as wife, mother and grandmother. Not only by her words, but also by her witness, Helen was and will continue to be an inspiration to Catholic women."

She was a good friend to many. I had the pleasure of knowing Helen and always found her, despite her many talents and accomplishments, to be most unassuming. At a conference for priests in Erie, Pennsylvania, she prefaced her talk by confessing that she was at a distinct disadvantage, especially addressing the clergy, because did not know a single joke. She prevailed upon one of the clergy, just prior to her presentation, to supply her with one. Thereupon she told her audience about a mother who came to the checkout counter with a package of diapers. "That will be $5 for the diapers and ten cents for the tax," said the clerk. "Oh no," replied the mother, "We don't use tacks, we use safety pins."

Helen, like so many women, was a person of great humor though not a joke teller. Nonetheless, she enjoyed a good witticism. We were talking to each other on the phone one time about the important role the mother plays in the moral education of her child. I fully agreed with her and said that if a child doesn't learn his moral values at his mother's knee, he will probably get them at some other joint. She laughed heartily and said, "That's good enough to invite you to our next convention." I always found it easy to get her to laugh.

She was an excellent draughtsman. Monsignor George William Rutler once informed an audience that Helen drew his portrait several times, revealing him in various stages of "decrepitude." Despite the seriousness of her work, people felt at home with her. Laughter and good cheer are infectious. She customarily signed memos about the Church in the United States to various officials in Rome, "HHH." No one would have confused her with Hubert Horatio Humphrey, though Helen had referred to the former presidential candidate in her writings. She and Cardinal Arinze were on the same program at Christendom College. When a friend barely uttered Hitchcock's name in introducing Helen to the

Cardinal, the then-prefect for the Congregation of Divine Worship and the Discipline of the Sacraments threw out his arms and exclaimed, "HHH!" Helen was thrilled to know that her memos were read in high Vatican circles.

In 1984, along with several other women, Helen Hull Hitchcock organized Women for Faith and Family, a movement of Catholic women which circulated the Affirmation for Catholic Women, a statement of fidelity to and unity with Church teachings. The affirmation has been signed by more than fifty thousand Catholic women throughout the world, including Saint Teresa of Kolkata. The affirmation has been translated into Spanish, Chinese, Dutch, Polish, French, Italian, and German.

HHH edited *The Politics of Prayer: Feminist Language and the Worship of God,* a collection of essays by various scholars.[55] Her superb introduction proves her to be a scholar among scholars. Moreover, her dedication to her parents is a thumbnail sketch of her life: "For my parents Downer Lee Hull and Thelma Kelly Hull, who taught me (and countless others) to speak, read, and esteem the English language—and through whose example I learned to love the Word of God." The lessons she learned from her parents and ancestors provided a solid ground in her eloquent defense of the Catholic Church against those who wanted to tear it apart. "As Catholics, who have been formed, inspired and sustained by the sacraments of the Church through participation in the liturgy," she wrote, "the Church's central action

---

[55]   Helen Hull Hitchcock, *The Politics of Prayer: Feminist Language and the Worship of God* (San Francisco: Ignatius Press, 1992).

and principal means of transmission of the Catholic faith, we are strongly aware of the power of symbol in human consciousness. We, therefore, deplore attempts to distort and transform language and liturgy, both of which make such potent symbolic impressions on the human mind, to confirm to a particular contemporary ideological agenda at odds with Catholic belief and practice."

Helen, along with twenty-six other converts to the Church of Rome, tell their conversion stories in *Spiritual Journeys: Twenty-Seven Men and Women Share Their Faith Experiences*.[56] Hers is an unbroken journey from the family farm in northern Kansas where members of seven generations of her family are buried to St. Louis, MO and the Church of Rome. She tells us of how her "discovery" of Thomistic philosophy was "intensely exhilarating, both intellectually and spiritually" and that she became a Catholic "because it is within the Catholic Church that I can affirm the Christian truth which I was taught as a child, and have believed, by the grace of God, all my life."

Helen published and edited *Voices*, Women for Faith and Family's quarterly journal, and *The Adoremus Bulletin*. The former has lapsed since her demise, though the latter, after a hiatus, is back in circulation under the guidance of a new editor. Fr. Joseph Fessio, SJ, once described this gentle soul as "a bulwark of the faith in the US." "But as I think of her now," he later added, "the refrain that I hear again and again is: 'well done, good and faithful servant.' Wife. Mother.

---

[56]   Robert Baram, *Spiritual Journeys: Twenty-Seven Men and Women Share Their Faith Experiences* (Boston, MA: St. Paul Editions, 1988).

Warrior. Journalist. Liturgist. Musician. Friend. Humorist. Helen."

Helen Hull Hitchcock's legacy is very much alive. This servant leader will continue to light the way for troubled Catholics and families that are searching for answers. She and her husband, Jim, the noted historian, have bequeathed to the world four daughters and six grandchildren.

Joan Andrews

I met Joan Andrews the day after she was released from prison at a pro-life conference in October 1988. She was friendly and cheerful. Her extended ordeal and denial of basic human rights had not, in the least, conquered her spirit. She had not had any food for a while and I offered to buy her something to eat. "No thanks," she said, munching on a candy bar. There were more important things on her mind.

I recall writing a letter to Joan's sister, Susan Brindle, suggesting that Joan has suffered enough for the unborn. Perhaps she should assist the cause in a way that is potentially less damaging to her. But Joan could not agree. She was a mother to all the unborn, and once you are a mother, she felt, you are always a mother. Joan was arrested more than 150 times for rescue-related actions and convicted sixty-seven times. But she never saw herself as either a hero or a saint. In one of her letters from prison, she writes, "I'm no saint, for one thing. I'm just a regular person who happened to be in the right place—or wrong place—to get arrested."

In March 1986, Joan Andrews, thirty-eight years old at the time, entered a Pensacola, Florida abortion center and tried, though unsuccessfully, to pull out the plug from a suction machine. The act seemed to be more symbolic than anything else. She was charged with burglary, malicious mischief, resisting arrest, and assault. In the state of Florida, the latter charge carries a life sentence. She remained in prison for four months under the threat of that sentence until it was dropped, simply because there was no basis for it. When she told the judge that she could not refrain from engaging in further, even legal, actions against abortion, she was denied bail.

After her conviction in a non-jury trial, she announced that "the only way I can protest for unborn children now is by non-cooperation in jail." Consequently, she was placed in solitary confinement and denied the right to attend Mass as part of her punishment. The judge sentenced her to five years in prison. Later that same day, he gave four-year sentences to two men who were convicted of accessory to murder.

When neither solitary confinement nor denying her the right to attend Mass failed to break her, she was transferred first to a medium security prison and then to Broward Correctional Institute in Miami, a maximum-security prison for Florida's most dangerous felons. A psychiatrist examined Joan and came to the conclusion that "she's not crazy or mentally ill. She simply has very strongly held beliefs. She's perfectly normal."[57]

---

[57]   Joan Andrews and Richard Cowden-Guido, *You Reject Them, You*

It was a travesty of justice that cried out to heaven. But it also cried out to the world. On Christmas Eve, 1987, nearly twenty thousand letters of protest were sent to Governor Martinez' office. The world had come to know about the barbaric treatment that Joan Andrews had received. Among her sympathetic supporters was none other than Mother Teresa of Calcutta: "You have offered all to God and accepted whatever you do to the least or for the least you do it to Jesus—because Jesus has clearly said, If you receive a little child in my name you receive Me."

Concerning the fact that she was illegally denied the right to attend Mass, an official stated rather tartly that "inmate Andrews is not in a state of sin because we will not allow her to participate in the Mass." As far as prison officials were concerned, Miss Andrew's cardinal sin was her non-cooperation.

In 1980, Joan lost her right eye to a fiercely malignant melanoma cancer. She wore a glass eye which required special care. Joan made weekly requests for a lubricant for that eye which was ignored for almost a year. As a result, she developed a series of sores around the eye socket. The word *martyr* means "witness." Joan was certainly a martyr for life. But she was also a witness to the breakdown of the American legal system. Jaime Cardinal Sin, Archbishop of Manila, once remarked that unjust prison sentences have often radically changed the direction of national or global affairs. "Take away the names of all the noble prisoners from history, and there will not be enough spiritual energy to run

---

Reject Me: The Prison Letters of Joan Andrews. Edited by Richard Cowden Guido (Manassas, Va: Trinity Communications, 1988).

the world." While Boethius was serving an unjust sentence in prison and awaiting his execution, he wrote *The Consolation of Philosophy* (c. 524) which is considered to be the single most important and influential work in the West on Medieval and early Renaissance Christianity. Joan may not have read this great work, but she did epitomize his notion that "joy is self-possession in the face of adversity."

Another victim of unjust imprisonment, closer to our era, is Rev. Martin Luther King. In his famous *Letter from a Birmingham Jail*, he refers to two types of laws: just and unjust: "I would be the first to advocate obeying just laws. . . . Conversely, one has a moral responsibility to disobey unjust laws. I would agree with St. Augustine that 'an unjust law is no law at all.' . . . To put it in terms of St. Thomas Aquinas: an unjust law is a human law that is not rooted in eternal law and natural law." How can you lose if you have Mother Teresa (now Saint Teresa of Kolkata), St. Augustine, St. Thomas Aquinas, Boethius, and Rev. Martin Luther King on your side?

Finally, Governor Martinez came on her side. By virtue of an executive order, he commuted Joan Andrews's sentence and she was released after serving thirty-one months, including twenty-six months in solitary confinement. She was given three years' probation. Joan is now married to a comparably zealous pro-lifer. They have one child born of their union and have adopted six others. Her witness continues to shine.

James McFadden

A small package was delivered to my office. It contained a copy of *The Human Life Review* and a note from its editor, James P. McFadden, inviting me, on the recommendation of an unnamed source, to write for his fledgling journal. I was honored by the invitation and soon dispatched an article which was just as soon rejected. There followed many additional submissions and an equal number of rejections. He became my coach, more than editor, urging me onward to better things, though occasionally expressing his frustrations with me. I had underestimated the standards set for HLR and, no doubt, overestimated my own abilities.

What writers were gracing the pages of McFadden's new journal? They were well-known personalities that established its high standards: Malcolm Muggeridge, Clare Boothe Luce, Jérôme Lejeune, President Ronald Reagan, Representative Henry Hyde, Senator James Buckley, Professors John T. Noonan and Paul Ramsey. High standards, indeed. A maxim dear to McFadden's heart was "Good writing can

win battles; great writing, whole wars." Could I ever be equal
to the task?

When I was in Manhattan, I stopped in to see him at his
East 35th St. office. "You are the most determined person I
have ever met," was his welcoming remark. In addition to
being perhaps the most patient person I had ever met, he
was most cordial and encouraging. He took me to lunch and
we discussed a wide assortment of things. Despite his New
York residence, he was an ardent fan of the Boston Red Sox.
The fact that we were both suffering at that time through
the "Curse of the Bambino" was an unexpected source of
bonding. He was addicted to puns, "The only certainties in
modern life," he said, "are death and faxes." Before I left, he
regaled me a tape of a May 21, 1979 testimonial given in his
honor, and a copy of John T. Noonan's latest book, *A Private
Choice*.[58] His generosity to me was repeated over the ensuing
years in many ways.

During my visit, he told me how he came to establish
the Human Life Foundation. Back in January of 1973, he
had been aboard William F. Buckley's yacht that docked in
Miami for repairs. Wanting to catch up on the news of the
day, he purchased a newspaper from a vending machine
and read the most disturbing news that the United States
Supreme Court had, by a vote of 7-2, ruled unconstitutional every one of the state laws that regulated the practice
of abortion and, at the same time, ruled that it was constitutional to hold that an unborn child was not a "person"

---

[58]   John T. Noonan, *A Private Choice, Abortion in America in the
Seventies* (New York: Free Press, 1979).

within its definition of that term, and that a woman had a constitutional "right to privacy" to abortion. Reading the horrifying news, McFadden there and then vowed to do something about it. Thus, the Human Life Foundation was born, together with *The Human Life Review* and other pro-life enterprises. The *Review* continues to flourish under the capable hands of Maria McFadden Maffucci. It is regarded as the "brains" of the pro-life movement.

James Patrick McFadden was the right man for the job. He had served for two years in military intelligence in Germany. He had the professional background, experience, and contacts required. And he knew a great deal about opinion journalism, publishing, direct mail, and other means of promotion. He was savvy as to how Washington worked and was well-versed in various political strategies. Moreover, he had the right temperament. *The Daily Telegraph* referred to him as "Clever, witty, rumbustious and religious" (October 28, 1998).

Thanks to his patience and guidance, I finally provided articles deemed worthy of appearing on the pages of *The Human Life Review*. McFadden was more than a mentor to me; he is an unforgettable character. He is, as his close friend William F. Buckley asserted, the "prime exhibit of G. K. Chesterton's dogged insistence that piety and laughter are inseparable, and indefeasibly the work of God." He had worked for thirty years as a journalist with Buckley's *National Review*. Malcolm Muggeridge said of him that "he combines to a remarkable degree a touch of saintliness and a strong dose of Machiavellianism—[comparable to] one of those drinks like gin and bitters that somehow work together very well." Jim could see the funny side of everything while remaining "deadly serious" about his faith, his family (there were five children), and his country.

Nonetheless, the perennial question arises: "Why do bad things happen to good people"? In 1993 Jim McFadden was diagnosed with the cancer that would ultimately take away his speech, his health, and his life. Surgery had removed his cancer but impaired his speech. Eventually, he lost completely his ability to speak. The cancer spread, first to the lungs, then to the colon and to the esophagus. Eighteen months later, his son, Robert, married just four years, died of cancer. Always a man of prayer, Jim would read the Psalms in the wee hours. One of his favorite passages was from Psalm 120: "In my distress I cry to the LORD, / that he may answer me: / 'Deliver me, O LORD, / from lying lips, / from a deceitful tongue.'"

Jim endured his suffering for five long years, though he remained motivated to the very end. He would get out of bed, attend seven o'clock Mass of St. Agnes church, and go to work. After editing *The Human Life Review* for twenty-four years, James Patrick McFadden passed from the earth on October 17, 1998 at the all-too-young age of sixty-eight. Journalist Ray Kerrison said of him that "life born and unborn, was everything to Jim. He defended it for others and fought desperately for it for himself. It was a privilege to know him" ("Death takes a stubborn defender of life," *New York Post*, October 22, 1998).

Kerrison may have gotten in the best final line when he wrote, in a Christmas card to McFadden's widow, Faith, "I can't help thinking how exasperated Jim must be in heaven.

Here he is, sitting on the greatest exclusive in all history—and he can't get the story out." Piety and laughter have a way of rubbing off on people.

Franz Jägerstätter

I was informed by a bishop recently that, according to reliable sources in the Vatican, approximately 100,000 Christians are martyred for their faith each year throughout the world. This is a most heart-rending statistic. At the same time, the blood of even one martyr can bring about much good.

Martyrdom means bearing witness to the Faith even unto death. It is the supreme witness that a person can give for the truth of his faith. The very etymology of the word (*martyros* in Greek) means "witness." The martyr accepts this death with courage as a witness to the Faith and to the presence of the kingdom of God.

The furthest thing from martyrdom is social respectability. The well-known writer Norman Cousins once denounced "any man in the pulpit who by his words and acts encourages his congregation to believe that the main purpose of the church or the synagogue is to provide social respectability for its members." A true Christian's faith is centered on Jesus, not polite society.

Martyrdom is the most definitive contradiction of "religion as hypocrisy." The fact of martyrdom is the ultimate and unequivocal witness, not of the world or of the self, but of God. It is the price that must be paid to silence the detractors and make the presence of God known to a world of skeptics and non-believers.

Franz Jägerstätter is a martyr for our modern world. His witness should be more widely known. Initially, a martyr, such as Jägerstätter, may be a "solitary witness." But there is no limit to the number of people who can be witnesses to his witness. Jägerstätter's witness might have remained "solitary" except for the witness of another—Catholic sociologist Gordon Zahn. It was Zahn, a University of Massachusetts professor, who discovered Jägerstätter's inspiring story of courage and unyielding commitment to God, and brought it to light in his book *In Solitary Witness*.[59] The book has now been translated into several languages, including German, French, Italian, and Greek.

Franz Jägerstätter was born in 1909 in St. Radegund, a small village in Upper Austria about thirty kilometers from Braunau-am-Inn, the birthplace of Adolph Hitler. In 1936 he married a woman from a nearby village, and the two went to Rome for their honeymoon. A Catholic by birth, Franz experienced a spiritual re-awakening of his faith around the

---

[59]   Gordon Charles Zahn, *In Solitary Witness: The Life and Death of Franz Jägerstätter* (Springfield, IL: Templegate Publishers, 1964).

time of his marriage and served his parish church in the capacity of a sexton.

On March 11, 1938, Hitler's forces crossed into Austria and two days later incorporated it into *Grossdeutschland*. In due time, the invaders presented Jägerstätter and all the other able-bodied men of St. Radegund their orders to swear allegiance to Hitler and serve in the Nazi army. Jägerstätter alone refused to comply. He was a Catholic, and in conscience could neither honor nor serve the evil purposes of an intrinsically immoral political regime. He refused, knowing that his refusal would cost him his life. The drama, in the words of Professor Zahn, was "nothing less than a repetition of an old story, the ever-recurring confrontation between Christ and Caesar."

Jägerstätter was married and a father to his wife's three little girls. He was also urged by many of his neighbors to be "prudent" and not risk his life by offending the Nazis. But Jägerstätter was resolved. While in prison and awaiting execution, he wrote, "Again and again people stress the obligations of conscience as they concern my wife and children. Yet I cannot believe that, just because one has a wife and children, he is free to offend God by lying (not to mention all the other things he would be called upon to do). Did not Christ Himself say, 'He who loves father, mother, or children more than Me is not deserving of My love?'" Just a few hours before his death, he stated in a letter to his family, "I will surely beg the dear God, if I am permitted to enter heaven soon, that he may also set aside a little place in heaven for all of you."

On August 9, 1943, in a Berlin prison, Franz Jägerstätter, like Saint Thomas More, was beheaded. The night before the execution, a Fr. Jochmann visited Jägerstätter in his cell. The priest found the prisoner, who had already received the last sacraments earlier that day, completely calm and prepared. The opportunity to avoid death was still available. On the table before him lay a document that Jägerstätter had only to sign in order to have his life spared. When the priest called his attention to it, Jägerstätter provided a simple explanation: "I cannot and may not take an oath in favor of a government that is fighting an unjust war."

Jägerstätter remained calm and composed when he walked to the scaffold. On that very same evening, Fr. Jochmann said, in the company of a group of Austrian nuns, "I can only congratulate you on this countryman of yours who lived as a saint and has now died a hero. I say with certainty that this simple man is the only saint that I have ever met in my lifetime."

Jägerstätter died convinced that his manner of death would pass unnoticed by the world and would completely fade from human memory with the passing of the handful of people who had known him personally. He was a martyr, not a prophet. In December 1984, responding to a nationwide petition, the president of Austria formally issued a special posthumous Award of Honor to Franz Jägerstätter. At the Second Vatican Council, an English archbishop called upon his fellow bishops "to consider this man [Franz Jägerstätter] and his sacrifice in a spirit of gratitude" and let his example "inspire our deliberations." The document that issued from these deliberations would be eventually known as *The Pastoral Constitution on the Church in the Modern World.*

Jägerstätter's example, one hopes, might inspire politicians to make acts of undying martyrdom by finding the courage to oppose the political pressure that obliges them to approve abortion, euthanasia, and other moral evils. To whom shall I be a witness is the most important decision a human being can ever make.

A LEAGUE OF HER OWN

Judie Brown

In the prologue of her autobiography, *It Is I Who Have Chosen You*, Judie Brown advises her readers that she is merely an ordinary person who is willing to be a servant of God.[60] Mother Angelica and Saint Teresa of Calcutta have said the same thing. Recognizing one's ordinariness, however, sets a person on the road to meaning since, as Mrs. Brown avers, "there is no aspect of life that is without purpose in God's plans. The title of her book comes from John 15:15–16: "I have called you friends, for all that I have heard from my Father I have made known to you. You did not choose me, but I chose you and appointed you."

While living in Kannapolis, North Carolina, she came face to face with her ordinariness in a most dramatic way. At the urging of her parish priest, she agreed to debate one of the most highly respected obstetrician/gynecologists in the area. She had no training in debating. Moreover, the only

---

60   Judie Brown, *It Is I Who Have Chosen You* (Stafford, VA.: American Life League, 1997).

pro-life experience she had had at that time was stuffing envelopes and carrying items to garage sales. She—pregnant with her third child, a housewife from a rental district in Kannapolis—was hardly an intimidating opponent for the learned doctor. When it was her turn to speak, she merely described what happens to a baby during an abortion. This so unnerved the doctor that he got up and walked out of the room. It was a re-run of the David and Goliath confrontation. She had similar encounters with TV host Phil Donohue and Faye Wattleton, president of Planned Parenthood.

Judith Ann Limbourne Brown was born in Los Angeles on March 4, 1944. She was a "breech" baby. As she would later say, "Even when I was still in the womb, I was giving others a challenge!" Her father abandoned the family a year and a half after Judie was born, leaving his wife and two young daughters to fend for themselves. Judie's maternal grandparents took the family in and made sure that Judie would receive a proper Catholic education. It was later revealed, unbeknownst to her mother, that she was her husband's fifth wife. In 1952, Judie's mother married Chester Limbourne.

After graduating from St. Mary's Academy in Inglewood, California, Judie Limbourne earned an Associate of Arts degree from a Junior College and, in 1965, completed her bachelor's degree program at UCLA. At age twenty-one she was an office manager at Kmart where she met her future husband, Paul Brown. They married on December 30, 1967.

On April 1, 1979, the Browns together with eight other pro-life Americans founded the American Life League (ALL). The purpose of the league was to educate the public about pro-life issues. Thanks to astute marketing and the assistance of a number of professionals in the field, ALL gained 68,000 members within its first year of existence. From a kitchen table operation, ALL has emerged as a full-fledged professional organization with more than thirty full-time employees and 120 associate organizations throughout the nation. The indefatigable Mrs. Brown, in addition to raising three children, found time to author a dozen books, including a critique of the American hierarchy: *The Broken Path: How Catholic Bishops Got Lost in the Weeds of American Politics.*[61] She and her husband currently look after their eleven grandchildren.

Judie Brown has written numerous articles for magazines and newspapers, including *The Washington Post* and *USA Today,* and has also appeared on numerous television programs, including *The Phil Donohue Show, 20/20, 60 Minutes, Mother Angelica Live, The O'Reilly Factor, Good Morning America, Oprah,* and *Larry King Live.*

The news from throughout the world concerning the advance of the Culture of Death supplies Mrs. Brown with more information than anyone can handle. Undaunted, however, she does her best in her twice-a-week columns to apprise her readers of what is going on, without the slightest concession to political correctness. In her May 10, 1917 column, she alerted people to the fact that in Australia, human embryos left over from in vitro fertilization as well as various embryo parts were being transformed into jewelry. She cited Amy McGlade, the company founder of

---

[61] Judie Brown, *The Broken Path: How Catholic Bishops Got Lost in the Weeds of American Politics* (Stafford, VA: American Life League, 2012).

Baby Bee Hummingbirds, who stated, "I don't believe there is any other business in the world that creates jewelry from human embryos, and I firmly believe that we are pioneering the way in this sacred art and opening the possibilities to families around the world." "Business enterprises like Baby Bee Hummingbirds," Judie Brown writes, "gain traction in society because the bearing of a child has become nothing more than a mechanical function. And that, my friends, has taken the jewelry business to a new hellish low." Mrs. Brown will never run out of grist for the mill, which includes some questionable statements and appointments made by none other than Pope Francis.

I count Judie Brown as a dear and valued friend, both personally and academically. She is unassuming, cordial, and dedicated. We were both corresponding members of the Pontifical Academy for Life. As editor of *Celebrate Life*, she has published many of my articles. As president of the American Life League, she invited me to be a member of her newly formed American Bioethics Advisory Commission and then supplied me with a generous flood of pertinent articles. She graciously responded when I invited her to write the foreword to *Architects of the Culture of Death* and promoted the book in *Celebrate Life* while offering the following challenge to its readers: "If you can finish this book and remain totally unchanged by what you learn, then you really didn't pay attention. Read it again."[62]

She is the recipient of numerous awards, perhaps the most

---

[62]   Donald DeMarco and Benjamin Wiker, *Architects of the Culture of Death* (San Francisco: Ignatius, 2004).

extravagant coming from the *Daily Catholic* that named Judie Brown forty-ninth on the list of "Top Catholics of the 20th Century." No doubt she found this selection rather amusing, if not laughable. Who in the world is in a position to create such a list? Nonetheless, given her resume for the current century, we may find, when the next such list comes out, that she may be moving up the ladder.

The Embattled Warrior

Joseph Scheidler

John Braine, author of *Room at the Top* and one of Britain's most successful novelists, provided a practical guide for aspiring novelists in his 1974 book *Writing a Novel.*[63] He advised that every novel should contain at least one highly improbable occurrence. I had never aspired to be a novelist but was fascinated by this bit of advice. Life itself is much larger than a novel. Therefore, extraordinary coincidences in life should happen more often than once.

I was at Chicago's O'Hare Airport waiting for my connecting flight. I thought to myself, "Who would I like to meet at this moment among the eight million or so people who reside in greater Chicago. I had a number of chance meetings with Joe Scheidler within recent memory and I thought I would like to meet him again. I awakened from my momentary reverie, looked up, and there he was—Joseph M. Scheidler in person—walking directly toward me. He

---

[63]   John Braine, *Room at the Top* (London: Eyre and Spottiswoode, 1957); John Braine, *Writing a Novel* (McGraw-Hill, 1975).

was not at all astonished by this remarkable coincidence and we passed the time discussing pro-life matters. I could not help thinking that providence had arranged this get-together for some special reason about which neither of us could be aware of at the time.

Joe Scheidler was born in Hartford City, Indiana in 1927. He earned a BA in journalism from Notre Dame and an MA in communications from Marquette. He spent four years as a Benedictine monk and eight years studying for the priest-hood. He left the seminary in 1959 thinking that he would have made a miserable priest if his bishop would not have allowed him to practice his strong anti-abortion beliefs. The last words his mother said to him on her deathbed at the age of eighty-two were, "Joe I'm so proud of your pro-life work. Keep it up." Scheidler and his wife, Ann, have seven children and numerous grandchildren.

In 1980, he founded the Pro-Life Action League that emphasized sidewalk counselling as perhaps the most effec-tive activity a pro-life person can perform. As a result, many women chose not to go through with their scheduled abor-tions and several abortion clinics were closed down. In 1985, his book *CLOSED: 99 Ways to Stop Abortion* was released.[64] "No social movement in the history of this country," he wrote in the introduction, "has succeeded without activists taking to the streets." Three different publishing houses were involved in its production: one to print it, a second to pub-licize it, and a third to correct ideological changes made by

---

64   Joseph M. Scheidler, *CLOSED: 99 Ways to Stop Abortion* (San Francisco, CA: Ignatius Press, 1985).

a feminist editor. *CLOSED* stresses courtesy, refraining from shouting back at hecklers, not blocking pedestrians or traffic, and not littering. It states that nine tenths of counselling is listening and insists that counsellors always provide a "peaceful presence." The approach is non-violent and respectful, but its mission is to save the lives of unborn babies.

By that time of the book's release, Scheidler had appeared on more than five hundred radio and television shows (including ABC-TV's "Nightline," the "MacNeill/Lehrer NewsHour," and the "Donohue Show"). His organization had 6,500 members working for him, most of whom were deeply committed to his brand of activism. He was as effective, though in ways that were always non-violent, as he was controversial. Political observer Thomas Roeser said of him that "it's not inaccurate to say he's the Martin Luther King of the time of the Montgomery bus boycott." Syndicated columnist Patrick Buchanan called the Pro-Life Action League "the Green Berets of the pro-life movement." At the same time, a priest accused him of Gestapo tactics.

But his real nemesis was the National Organization of Women. In 1998, a federal court decided against Scheidler and in favor of NOW. He was found guilty of interstate racketeering, assessed fines, and sentenced to prison. The United States Supreme Court, however, unanimously overturned the decision in 2003. Undeterred, NOW once again filed a suit against Scheidler that was upheld by another federal court. However, the Supreme Court once again, in 2006, unanimously ruled in Scheidler's favor, granting him damages against NOW.

The initial lawsuit against Scheidler, involving the RICO

amendment, was curious. The US Federal Racketeering Influenced and Corrupt Organizations Act (RICO) of 1970 was originally written to target organized crime. It allowed courts to attack "enterprises" that engage in a "pattern of racketeering." Scheidler and his Pro-Life Action League, which is a non-profit organization, could hardly have been classified as a "racketeering enterprise" under the RICO amendment.

I first met Joe Scheidler at the Hyatt Regency hotel in Washington, DC. I recognized him from his photographs and my first words to him were, "You're Joe Scheidler." "What's left of me," he quipped. There was the embattled warrior. But certainly undefeated and not without a sense of humor. His motto, taken from Cardinal Newman, was to treat one's enemies as if they would one day become your friends. He believed in the possibility of people changing their minds and hearts. He fervently believed that justice can prevail over injustice, truth over falsity, and ethics over impulse.

Since 1980, Scheidler has spoken in more than one thousand towns and cities, in forty-eight of the fifty states. Abroad, he has conducted on-site workshops and lectures in Canada, Italy, Australia, New Zealand, and Ireland. He has been as indefatigable as he has been determined.

Scheidler's activities provide a litmus test that reveals the moral state of the nation. Abortion divides the country into parties that are so morally distant from each other that they no longer employ a common language. The abortion issue reveals that America has become a nation of strangers. The notion that the National Organization of Women, for whom motherhood should be prized as a blessing, can accuse a pro-life group, whose only concern is to save lives, of consisting of gangsters demonstrates the depth of this division. Also revealed is the shocking disparity in thinking that exists within the judicial system. To commit oneself to life and justice, as Scheidler does, is to put your own life at risk and assume the possibility of becoming a victim of injustice. Scheidler fought the great battle and won. We can thank him and, as much as we are able, follow in his footsteps.

Happily, we can be inspired in doing so by reading his recently published memoirs, *Racketeer for Life*, published by TAN Books.[65]

---

[65]   Joseph M. Scheidler, *Racketeer for Life: Fighting the Culture of Death from the Sidewalk to the Supreme Court* (Charlotte, NC: TAN Books, 2016).

THE HOLY FAMILY

Jesus, Joseph, and Mary

In Christian parlance, Christmas is rightly celebrated as the Nativity. It is not Father's Day or Mother's Day, but the day when the child Jesus was born. This may seem to be an unnecessary or even trivial observation, but it actually represents an important insight into why the Holy Family is so named.

The ancient notion of *pater familias* (the Latin expression for "father of the family," or "owner of the family estate") placed the father first, the mother a distant second, and the child a far distant third. With regard to the Holy Family, the order is reversed so that the child comes first, the mother second, and the father third. Thus, Christmas, first and foremost, is about the child Jesus. Mary is never absent from the child, but she does not dominate the spotlight. In all the icons of the Mother of God, Mary's eyes are always drawn to her child. St. Joseph is present, but clearly in third place. Joseph protects, Mary nourishes, but Jesus is the fulfillment.

The pope is also known as the Holy Father. Pope (*papa*

in Italian) means "father." When Pope Gregory the Great gave himself the title of *Servus servorum Dei* (servant of the servants of God), he did not abandon his role as pope and spiritual leader of the Church, but he made it clear that not he, but others come first. The paradox here is that the leader subordinates himself in love for others so that he can be a better leader. The proud man thinks primarily of himself; the humble man thinks first of others. In stark contrast with King Herod, Catholic popes have consistently adopted the role that Pope Gregory bequeathed to them.

The modern family in the secular world prefers a different order than that which characterizes the Holy Family. It gives a place of supremacy to the mother while demoting the child to third place, a reduction in value that opens the door to abortion, child neglect, and the increasing popularity of marriages that are childless by choice. The father is often regarded as an unnecessary or bothersome appendage. Contraception, abortion, and divorce are common. This is the "profile" of the modern "unholy family," which is not in accord with its "pro-life" anagrammatic companion.

If we seek the reasons to explain the holiness of the Holy Family, we find one in the unchecked transmission of love that begins with God, flows through Joseph and Mary, and culminates in the child. Love has a forward motion. It overcomes obstacles. "*Amor omnia vincit*" (love conquers all) as the Romans said. Happiness characterizes those who live by love. And "happiness expresses itself as the desire to reproduce the beautiful," as Plato stated. This applies very well to the Holy Family and any other family that aspires to holiness. In addition to the uninterrupted flow of love, there are the other supernatural virtues, faith and hope, that mark the holiness of the Holy Family. Mary needed faith to believe that she, despite her virginity, would bear the Christ child. She needed hope to be assured that she would be an effective instrument in the unfolding of God's plan.

The decision to abort may be the consequence of a lack of love. Moreover, it may be influenced by a lack of faith that the pregnancy will go well. Or it could be a lack of hope that the child will be healthy and lead a meaningful life. A family that is deficient in love, faith, or hope places the child at risk and is not modelling itself after the Holy Family.

In 1643, Louise and Barbe d'Ailleboust came to Canada with the purpose of devoting their lives to the welfare of the natives. After the death of her husband, Barbe, she founded, with the help of the Jesuit Father Chaumonot, the Confraternity of the Holy Family, which spread throughout the country. Her work drew the attention of Monsignor François Laval who established the feast of the Holy Family. The feast was added on October 26, 1921, under Pope Benedict XV, to the general calendar of the Western Rite with the purpose of counteracting the breakdown of the family. Bishop Laval was canonized on April 3, 2014 by Pope Francis. Today, the Church celebrates the Feast of the Holy Family on the Sunday that falls between Christmas and New Year's Day (or on December 30 when there is no Sunday between those dates).

The Holy Family is the model family for all other families inasmuch as it perfectly integrates the supernatural virtues of love, faith, and hope. It is a most appropriate model in today's world when the family is suffering acutely, not only from forces from without but also from forces from within.

At the close of his apostolic exhortation *The Role of the Family in the Modern World*, Saint John Paul II prays to St. Joseph that he may "always guard and protect and enlighten families," and to Mary that she may "be an example of humble and generous acceptance of the will of God" and "comfort the sufferings and dry the tears of those in distress because of the difficulties of their families." He invokes the help of the Holy Family to help ailing families, mindful of the fact that the future of humanity passes through the family. In his sermon on the Feast of the Holy Family (Sunday, December 20, 1978), he reiterated, in accordance with Vatican II, that "the deepest human problems are connected with the family. It constitutes the primary, fundamental and irreplaceable community for man."

G. K. Chesterton, in *The Everlasting Man*, contrasts the Holy Family with the mere human family with his characteristic clarity, conciseness, and humor: "The old Trinity was of father and mother and child and is called the human family. The new is of child and mother and father and has the name of the Holy Family. It is in no way altered except in being entirely reversed; just as the world which is transformed was not in the least different, except in being turned upside-down."

The Holy Family, then, is a Trinity of Apostles for Life.

About the Author

Dr. Donald T. DeMarco is the author of more than thirty books and has been an editorial advisor and a regular columnist for several publications. Dr. DeMarco has served as a Corresponding Member of the Pontifical Academy for Life and, from his home in Canada, for thirty years as president of his local Birthright. A long-time professor of philosophy, he earned his PhD at St. John's University in New York. Dr. DeMarco also has the good sense and fortune to be a fan of Boston sports teams.